FIND YOUR PURPOSE IN 15 MINUTES WORKBOOK

Your Shortcut to a Meaningful Life

-A *Nourish Your Soul* Workbook-

Julie Schooler

Copyright © 2022 Julie Schooler, BoomerMax Ltd

ISBN: 978-0-473-65521-1

All rights reserved. No part of this publication may be reproduced, distributed, or transmitted in any form or by any means, including photocopying, recording, or other electronic or mechanical methods, without the prior written permission of the publisher, except in the case of brief quotations embodied in reviews and certain other non-commercial uses permitted by copyright law.

DISCLAIMER

This book is designed to give readers some useful tips and ideas. It does not replace expert advice from medical or behavioral specialists. It is recommended that you seek advice from qualified professionals if you are concerned in any way.

This book is dedicated to my smart, strong and beautiful three-year-old, Eloise, who has absolutely no problem saying 'NO!'

CONTENTS

Reader Gift: The Happy20	ix
1. Despair to Delight	1
2. Why Are You Here?	9
3. Purpose Questions (and a Wee Rant)	19
4. Purpose Answers	25
5. Find Your Purpose in 15 Minutes	35
6. Plant Your Purpose in Your Mind, Heart and Soul	53
7. Purpose in the Real World	61
8. Diving Deeper: Tests	71
9. Diving Deeper: Questions	85
10. Diving Deeper: Exercises	101
11. Supercharge Your Purpose	113
12. What is the Purpose of a Book on Purpose?	119
Appendix One – Find Your Purpose in 15 Minutes Summary	125
Appendix Two – My Test Results	129
Appendix Three – My Obituary Exercise	131
Reader Gift: The Happy20	133
About the Author	135
Books By Julie Schooler	137
Acknowledgments	139
Please Leave a Review	141
References	143

READER GIFT: THE HAPPY20

There is no doubt that having a purpose will transform your life, but it is also important to remember to squeeze the best out every single day. To remind you of this, I created

The Happy20
20 Free Ways to Boost Happiness in 20 Seconds or Less

A PDF gift for you with quick ideas to improve your mood and add a little sparkle to your day.

Head to **JulieSchooler.com/gift** and grab your copy today.

1

DESPAIR TO DELIGHT

 'Tell me, what is it you plan to do with your one wild and precious life?' – Mary Oliver

THE WORLD IS ON FIRE

- Do you feel like your life is going nowhere?
- Do you struggle to get out of bed each morning?
- Do you want your life be meaningful but don't know where to start?

More than ever, people all over the world are feeling disillusioned and disempowered. In Western countries many of us are fortunate to have plenty of material comforts, but statistics show that we are unhappier than we have ever been.

We are told that finding our purpose, our WHY, is the solution to thinking life is pointless. It is declared that discovering the meaning of our lives can help us feel less lost, eliminate our feelings of despair and make our day-to-day lives full of hope instead of drudgery.

BUT…

Finding a purpose looks too difficult to do, seems to take forever to work out and implies that our whole lives will have to change even if we somehow do manage to attempt this arduous task.

We are STUCK as we know we can't go on living this way without a purpose, BUT we are not sure how to find one.

No wonder the world feels like it is at a crisis point. No wonder we all eat too much, sit too much and binge watch too much. It's amazing that anyone gets out of bed in the morning at all!

The Purpose Solution

Find Your Purpose in 15 Minutes delivers a handy tool to help you discover your ideal life purpose in a matter of minutes.

This book will give you:

- A definition for purpose that is simple to understand and start from
- An easy-to-use template to write out your ideal purpose statement
- A 15-minute exercise that creates your purpose step-by-step
- An ideal purpose that feels profoundly significant and unique to you

You will not only find your purpose but also learn how to use it in your life. You will learn ways to LIVE it even if you don't know where to start or are afraid of change. This book will give strategies to help you to incorporate your newfound purpose seamlessly into your life and effortlessly stay the course.

This entertaining and easy-to-read guide will also cut through the confusion around what meaning, purpose, destiny and 'a calling' really are, provide compelling reasons why finding your purpose adds an uplifting element to your life and tells you exactly what to do to supercharge your purpose—even if you have never thought about any of these aspects before. If you enjoy the quick introspection during the purpose exercise, there is also the option of doing some extra tests, questions and exercises that help you understand and appreciate yourself on a deeper level.

You won't need to spend hours searching for information all over the Internet. You will have a clear direction and won't be confused by conflicting advice. This book will give you the exact blueprint to writing your own purpose in a way that feels like you have known it all along. Your purpose will help you spring out of bed every morning with renewed enthusiasm for living, not just existing.

How Finding My Purpose Helps YOU

Like you, I want my life to feel meaningful and worthwhile, so I spent a long, long time trying to figure out my ultimate purpose. I read lots of books, researched the topic extensively and went to many motivational seminars and personal development events.

I thought that something this significant should take serious contemplation plus long hours trying to understand my intuitive desires, childhood wishes and visions of my ideal future.

BUT....

Recently I had an epiphany: why does it need to be so difficult?

The more important thing is LIVING with purpose. If I could just eliminate the so-called hard part of working it out, I could swiftly start maneuvering my life in the right direction.

I distilled the avalanche of information and all my learnings into a simple and fun fool-proof formula to find my purpose. Then I got on with the more important job: starting to live it.

Finding my purpose in 15 minutes helped me to structure my life better, say 'no' to the unimportant and feel renewed energy when the perfect project for me came my way. It gave me clarity, simplicity and freedom. I find it amazing that one short statement can convey so much power.

It was obvious to me that many people could use this life shortcut to help them with both their day-to-day and their big picture decisions so they too could feel like they were working towards a destiny.

I could not find one short, clear, gimmick-free guide on how to find your purpose in this way, so I wrote one. This book contains all the tools, advice and inspiration you need to find and live your purpose in a way that makes your heart sing.

I have written the book that I wanted to read.

Purpose Rewards

Just think how great it will be when you find your purpose in 15 minutes. There are benefits in so many areas. You will:

- understand your true self better
- rediscover buried desires and drivers
- feel good about yourself for having a clear path
- know the direction to follow to get what you want
- lead and inspire others to live life on their own terms
- wake up each morning with a sense of excitement and zest for life
- feel like you are living the life you were meant to live, one with meaning and true joy

Purpose Praise

Busy people are happy to recommend this book as it contains everything they need and nothing they don't to easily discover their purpose in life. They are excited that there is a finally a short book that helps them to effortlessly write and take action on a clear meaning for their lives.

Readers are excited that there is finally a fun and easy-to-read book that removes any stigma that finding your purpose has to be serious, take a long time or that your life has to change in a dramatic way.

Early volunteers who took the 'Find Your Purpose in 15 Minutes' questionnaire had overwhelmingly positive feedback. They loved the opportunity to take some time to reflect on their lives, found the exercise short and sweet and were surprised something so simple could feel so profound. Many said they felt uplifted, empowered and inspired to live well.

This is just one of many amazing comments: "This is very insightful and I wish I had done it a long time ago. It's comforting and liberating at the same time. It makes all the noise fall away and provides that clarity we are always looking to find."

Purpose Promise

This book will make it exciting and easy to rediscover your purpose. This is the most stress-free and light-hearted book on finding your purpose you will ever read.

You will write your purpose so clearly and ingrain it so deeply you can recite it in your sleep. Plus it will get you bouncing with a joy of life you had forgotten you had.

In addition, I promise that you will have simple yet uplifting tools for bringing your life in line with your purpose without having to sell your house, ditch your family or move to a mountain in Nepal!

It is guaranteed that if you use this book to write your purpose, you will feel enthused about life once again, you will have less to worry about, and you will give yourself the best gift of all—a clear path to designing your destiny.

Find Your Purpose Today

Do not wait until you snooze another alarm clock buzzer over and over as you struggle to get out of bed. Read this book and add some much needed clarity, direction and fun back into your life. Find your purpose so you can immediately start to improve your health, relationships and work. Why postpone being happier?

A Simple Way to Shine

Find Your Purpose in 15 Minutes plucks out what is important to you, what you love, what you are good at and what you can give and easily inputs them into an ideal purpose statement just for you.

This book proves that finding your purpose - your WHY - can be fun, quick and simple. It CAN be a delight, if you let it. Plus it confirms how enriching it can be to weave your purpose into your life. Why not give yourself the gift of finding YOUR purpose today?

There is a light inside of you that has been dimmed for far too long.

Let the world see you shine.

WORKBOOK NOTE

In each chapter of this workbook there will be questions and prompts so that you can write down your answers, notes and ideas that are designed to help you find your purpose. Feel free to write as much or as little as you like. You can even skip sections. But please, no matter what, follow and complete the Find Your Purpose in 15 Minutes *exercise in Chapter 5 to find your life's purpose.*

2

WHY ARE YOU HERE?

 'Why stop now just when I'm hating it?' – Marvin, the paranoid android from *The Hitchhiker's Guide to the Galaxy*

The Answers

For thousands of years people have been asking questions centered on purpose: "What is the meaning of life?", "Why are we here?", "What is the purpose of MY life?".

The answers to these questions are even more varied than the questions themselves. They can be found amongst the ideas of ancient philosophers, in scientific theories, part of faith-based beliefs and even in popular culture.

Philosopher, Aristotle, fundamentally linked happiness to the meaning of life. Astrophysicist, Neil deGrasse Tyson says we create our own meaning, and many faith-based explanations associate a meaningful life with a relationship to a higher power.

Pop culture has even added its two cents: in the *Hitchhiker's Guide to the Galaxy* book series, the main characters finally discover the "answer to the ultimate question of life, the universe and everything" is, bizarrely, 42.

And no summary of questions and answers about purpose can be complete without this gem from the Monty Python film, *The Meaning of Life*, in which the answer is read out from an envelope as: "try to be nice to people, avoid eating fat, read a good book every now and then, get some walking in, and try to live together in peace and harmony with people of all creeds and nations."

No one agrees exactly on the meaning of life.

And that is great news for you!

Now you have a blank slate on which to discover YOUR purpose for YOUR life. It doesn't actually matter what the meaning is for "life, the universe and everything".

What is important is finding out YOUR purpose in life and then LIVING it.

Who This Book is For

So are you in the right place? If you are between 9 and 90 and nod your head at any of these statements, then you are in the perfect spot:

- You would love a simple, fast and robust method of finding your purpose.
- You are in a funk and want a quick way of refocusing your life on something more positive and meaningful.
- You haven't really thought about finding your purpose until now but sometimes do wonder about why you are here or what is life about.

Chapter Five invites you to find your purpose in 15 minutes, and I fully expect some eager readers to head straight there! I do suggest to get your mindset in order before launching into the 15-minute exercise and first read the next couple of chapters that explain why you have not found your purpose before now and then discover why it is mission critical to do so.

Once you find your purpose in 15 minutes you may be thinking "What now?" This book will show you how you can make your newfound purpose an integral part of your life—even if your current day-to-day looks nothing like it. It also gives suggestions on how to calibrate with your purpose when you go out of alignment and what to do with the naysayers who don't like the new purpose-driven you.

If you enjoyed the chance to reflect and dream and want to go further, there are some interesting and thought-provoking tests, questions and exercises so you can find out even more about how you tick and what is truly important to the real you. The book wraps up with a few suggestions to supercharge your new, purposeful life.

Why I Wrote This Book

Other than the fact that it seems like one of the most significant things we as humans have the privilege of contemplating, why write a book on finding your purpose?

To be ridiculously honest with you, the first reason is because I am turning 42 this year. Yes, the favorite pop culture answer to the meaning of life created an impetus to write a book on purpose.

It also seemed like the next logical step after publishing a book on goal setting. The trouble was that in *Super Sexy Goal Setting*, I advised readers to skip over the step of finding their life purpose before setting goals as I thought it would take too much time and may even stop the more important task of goal setting completely.

I was also drawn towards writing a book on purpose as I was fortunate to attend Tony Robbins' Date with Destiny event earlier this year. During the six grueling but phenomenal days we did a lot of work on ourselves to discover who we truly are and what our ideal lives would look like if we erased our fears and limiting beliefs and reached for the stars. We ended the event writing a mission statement for our dream lives. Look, the event was amazing, BUT it took us six days to get to our purposes! Six days!

This is my key issue with finding your purpose and why I advised against it in *Super Sexy Goal Setting*. In all the research I did, finding your purpose always seemed to take hours of contemplating about your childhood, or your ideal life or what legacy you want to leave. Many guides I read on the topic wanted me to tap into my intuition and discover what my soul was telling me my life purpose was. Look, I love a bit of woo-woo, but when it comes to finding my life purpose, I didn't want to rely on my fickle and often absent intuition, my poor memory of my childhood wishes or my dismally unimaginative vision of a future me.

I loved every minute at Date with Destiny, but the whole experience provoked me to reconsider my belief that finding my purpose had to take ages. After the event, I asked myself a radical question: instead of a few days could someone be prompted to work out his or her purpose in a few minutes?

I wanted a simple, practical tool that could spell out a life purpose in a quick and easy way. I wanted to figure out what my life purpose was in the shortest amount of time and then get on with the more important job—living it.

And I wanted to help as many people as possible do this, too.

Definitions

Look, I am sorry, I hate to do this, but we all must get clear on the main terms in this area, otherwise things can get downright confusing.

Purpose of life: There are many definitions of purpose, so I have used a widely accepted understanding. Your life purpose is your WHY for being here. It is what you live for, what is important to you and what makes your life significant and worthwhile. This book will use 'purpose', 'your purpose', 'life purpose' or 'purpose of life' interchangeably.

Meaning of life: This is almost the same as 'purpose of life', although it seems to have a broader reach. People often ask what is the purpose of MY life and what is the meaning of life in general.

Destiny: The simple meaning of destiny is the things that will happen in the future including what you will do and the type of person you will be. 'Destiny' can sometimes imply that your future is decided by and controlled by a powerful and mysterious force.

Fate: Very similar to destiny, 'fate' can simply mean what happens to a person. It can also be extended to mean a power that controls events so they cannot be changed. It is often associated with an adverse outcome or death.

Dream: A dream is something amazing that you want to happen or you hope to achieve in the future but may be considered hard or unlikely.

Calling: A calling is a strong impulse to a course of action especially if there is a conviction it will be socially valuable. It is mostly connected with being attracted to a profession, career or work that helps others.

Vision: A vision is an idea or plan for the future. It is usually related to a specific organization or project.

Mission: An aim that is very important or a strong commitment to do or achieve something. Sometimes a purpose statement is called a mission statement.

Legacy: Something that has been achieved or exists after a person stops working or dies. Ultimately it is the thing for which you will be remembered.

In summary, purpose can also be interchanged with the words 'meaning', 'vision' and 'mission', and at a stretch it could be suggested with the words 'destiny', 'fate', 'calling' and 'legacy'.

No wonder no one tries to find his or her purpose! Just navigating the language around it is difficult enough. Never mind. Let's move on.

Parts of Purpose

Purpose is your big picture WHY, your highest reason for being here. To create a short, positive and powerful purpose statement, use this simple formula:

Your purpose is about who you want to BE and what you want to DO so that you have an IMPACT on others.

Your purpose statement is written using this template:

> 'The purpose of my life is to (be and/or do) _____ to (impact) _____'.

The BE and DO part is self-enhancing. It is the passions, strengths and values you have or aspire to embody. **Passions** are sometimes confused with purpose but are not the same. A passion is something you are strongly interested in, what you love to do, what you enjoy or what excites you. The root of the word comes from the Latin 'passio' meaning 'to suffer', so it implies you care so deeply that it hurts. If this seems a little too intense, then just think of what you like to do or what you are curious about. **Strengths** are talents or abilities that you have. Things that you are good at, that you would be able to teach to someone or qualities that give you an advantage or make you more effective. **Values** are what you care about, what matters most to you and what you stand for. Values are principles and emotional states that are important to you. There is a lot of overlap between these three areas.

The IMPACT part is self-transcending. This contribution aspect makes your purpose greater than a goal with its focus on your relationship to, sharing of your gifts with or impact on others (all others or a particular group).

SOURCES

Although this is merely one interpretation of what purpose is and one way to write out a purpose statement, it is based on a lot of research on this topic. Here are some of the main sources of how this purpose statement was developed:

- Positive psychology: describes a meaningful life as using your strengths in the service of something larger than you
- Bluezones: researchers who study the healthiest and longest living communities define purpose as a cross section between what your values are, what you like to do, what you are good at and what you have to give
- Victor Frankl, a holocaust survivor who wrote the bestseller, *Man's Search for Meaning* saw three possible sources of meaning—work (doing something significant), love (caring for another) and in courage during difficult times
- Jack Canfield, author of *Success Principles,* states that "Ultimately our purpose is to serve each other with the expression of who we are in the world."
- In the book *The Top Five Regrets of the Dying*, overall what mattered most to the dying was how much happiness they

- brought to those they loved and how much time they spent doing things they loved
- Mike Sherbakov from The Greatness Foundation states that your purpose is the intersection of what you are passionate about, what you are good at and your connection to the world—what problems you want to fix
- In research, three factors stood out as predictors of happy 100-year-olds—the ability to get over disappointment, an outward view of life (caring about others and being involved positively in society) and a passion that is actively pursued

My Purpose Statement

Chapter Five provides the step-by-step instructions plus the top BE, DO and IMPACT words that can be slotted into the purpose template to help you easily write your ideal purpose statement in minutes.

Before that, dive a bit deeper into why you haven't tried to find your purpose in life up until now, get answers to some of the main questions you may have on finding your purpose, plus understand some of the benefits of a purpose-driven life.

At the end of each chapter you will be able to read some real life purpose statements generously supplied by a tribe of early volunteers of this 15-minute purpose exercise. Some statements are very short, some are long, some fit into this template strictly and some use it as a jumping off point to develop their perfect purpose. All are different and reflect the unique true self of the individual. I am full of deep gratitude to these life purpose guinea pigs. Thank you so much for your time and feedback.

To kick things off, here is my purpose statement:

> Julie: *The purpose of my life is to be my best self, full of love, energy and fun ('sparkle'), so I can continue to learn and create and then inspire others to achieve their potential.*

WHY ARE YOU READING THIS BOOK?

What attracted you to this book? Would you like to understand exactly how to find your purpose? Do you want to create a purpose statement from scratch or revise one you already have started? Perhaps you need more ideas or prompts to start finding your purpose? Write down why you are here. Know that no matter what, you are in the right place.

_____

_____

_____

_____

_____

_____

_____

_____

_____

3

PURPOSE QUESTIONS (AND A WEE RANT)

 'Life's but ... a tale told by an idiot, full of sound and fury, signifying nothing.' – William Shakespeare's *Macbeth*, spoken by Macbeth

OBJECTION QUESTIONS

Finding your life purpose can be confrontational. Here are some of the main objections to attempting to figure out a purpose in life in the form of questions:

> My life has been good without knowing my purpose, so why should I?
> What if I figure out my purpose and my life doesn't reflect it at all?
> What is the point of the 'find your life purpose' exercise again?
> What if I write out my purpose statement and it is not 'right'?
> Do I really have to figure out the purpose of my life?
> Won't it take up too much time to get an answer?

If I had a purpose, wouldn't I just know it?
Isn't it a lot of hard work, and for what?
Can my life purpose be changed?
Does everyone have a purpose?
Do I have to change my life?
What is the point of it all?

WHAT IS THE POINT OF IT ALL?

The answers to these questions are in the next chapter. But why do we have so many objections to finding our purpose?

A lot of it stems from not being sure life has any meaning at all. If life has no meaning, then there seems to be zero point trying to extract out a purpose for our lives from our meaningless existence.

There is no real reason to think there is any purpose or meaning to our brief time here on Earth. We are merely an accident of time, space, and matter. We came to be through chaotic processes of physics and evolution, which is great for us, but essentially meaningless.

The universe is estimated to be about 91 billion light years in diameter. Think long and hard about that. Light travels at 186,000 miles per second. It takes eight minutes just for sunlight to reach Earth. Try and picture just how enormous 91 billion light years is. You can't.

We live on a little spinning planet in the middle of a solar system on the edge of a galaxy tucked into a corner of a vast universe. Imagine how trivial we are—our small galaxy, our tiny solar system, our miniscule planet. We could not be more insignificant in the greater scheme of things. In this gigantic swirling void of mostly nothingness, humans are but motes of stardust.

Many people seem to be just marking time—fidgeting between "the maternity ward and crematorium" as British philosopher, Alan Watts, aptly puts it. For most of us our day-to-day struggles to be a good person and to do well in the world will be forgotten and irrelevant in a period of mere months or years.

None of us is immortal. Each of us has maybe 100 years to make our mark, to do something with our lives. It doesn't seem like much time to create meaning. Death is inevitable yet terrifying, as despite our best efforts to believe in something beyond it, no one knows for sure. According to anthropologist and writer, Ernest Becker, this deep existential anxiety underlies everything we do, so any meaning we attempt our life to have is shaped by this innate desire to never die.

Hence many try to create a lasting legacy. You are one of around seven billion people currently alive, so how can anything you do truly matter? Very few of us will do anything in our lives that will have any importance beyond our own life spans and our own friends and families. A few people will do something that changes our world, but even Albert Einstein, Nelson Mandela and Beyoncé will eventually be forgotten. These children we work so hard to raise are going to die, too, as will their children and so on. What is the point of making an impact, anyway? Trying to do so feels at worst fruitless and, at best, like littering.

It is a tendency of humankind to think that we must somehow be very important because we have sentience and civilization (such as it is) and symphony orchestras and great art and the Internet and whatnot, and it seems too amazing to have occurred by chance. But we are just bags of skin with trillions of bugs inside of us. Bugs similar to the type that will be on the planet long after the zombie apocalypse wipes us all out and we are all gone.

When even our briefest of time here on Earth is ridiculous, absurd and nonsensical, how can we extract any kind of purpose from it? How can a 15-second video of a rat transporting a slice of pizza down some stairs get over 8.5 million views, while human slavery be a bigger problem than it was 150 years ago? How can it be possible to order a burger via emojis, but there not be safe, clean drinking water available for everyone? What sort of world do we live in where news coverage centers on the Kardashian clan and the silly names they have given their children rather than the fact that topsoil and tigers are disappearing and the oceans are filling up with titanic amounts of plastic waste?

Life doesn't owe you anything. The universe does not care about you. The universe is mostly a freezing void. Eventually the sun will expand and swallow our planet and we will become extinct. Even if we have mastered interstellar travel (unlikely) the universe will eventually collapse upon itself. Nothing lasts.

To sum up: The universe is big and we are small. When you look at the size of universe and the expanse of time, nothing we ever do in our lives has any point at all.

Any way we look at it, life is insignificant, meaningless and absurd.

And a good day to you, sir.

Sunset Prescription

Wowsers, where did that all come from?

You are one tough, nihilistic-tasting cookie!

I prescribe taking a few deep breaths plus a mandatory viewing of the nearest sunset, stat!

In the next chapter we will address the objection questions and tell you why you absolutely NEED a purpose.

Purpose Statements

Carrie: *The purpose of my life is to be kind, positive and enjoy so that I can be brave, learn to teach and make a difference to my community.*

Ton: *To be a safe haven in order to ease suffering of all sentient beings.*

Lisa: *The purpose of my life is to be joyful and energetic, to be confident and always growing so I can inspire and empower others to create a life they love.*

Julia: *The purpose of my life is to grow! To grow in knowledge but also to grow food to feed people and contribute and to grow a peaceful garden farm and environment to better people, animals and nature.*

Additional Notes

This is HEAVY stuff! Write down anything that has come up for you after reading this chapter.

_____

_____

_____

_____

_____

4

PURPOSE ANSWERS

> *'This is the true joy in life, being used for a purpose recognized by yourself as a mighty one. Being a force of nature instead of a feverish, selfish little clod of ailments and grievances, complaining that the world will not devote itself to making you happy.'* – George Bernard Shaw

Objection Answers

Is there any way to overcome the notion that all life is meaningless? The answers to the main objections will help you to see another perspective and lead you to being excited about finding your purpose in the next chapter.

My life has been good without knowing my purpose, so why should I?

Worried you may upset the apple cart of your perfectly acceptable life? But you wouldn't be here if you weren't a little curious about how brilliant your life could be. After all, no matter how great our lives are, there is another level—one of passion, beauty, connection, energy and happiness.

I said it in *Super Sexy Goal Setting* and I will say it again: you owe it to the world to use up every single tiny ounce of all the resources and riches with which you were so fortunately bestowed to reach your potential, create value and share your gifts with the world. It would be a travesty if you just settled because you thought you didn't deserve even more from life.

What if I figure out my purpose and my life doesn't reflect it at all?

People find it intimidating to think about finding their purpose as it is very clear whether they are living it. Your purpose is a filter that you now can't ignore.

Don't worry if you find your purpose and your life looks nothing like it! You certainly don't have to ditch your current life. Knowing your purpose will give you some clarity around what you want and why you want it. It will help you say 'yes' to things that support it, and easily—and in a guilt-free way—say 'no' to things that have no place in your purpose-aligned life. Some people will find that their lives slowly ease into line with their purpose without a lot of effort. Others may make some drastic changes.

We will address this later, so please don't make it an excuse not to find your purpose at all. You can still find your purpose and start to use it as a guiding light, something to aspire to. And what if your life already DOES reflect your purpose?

Wouldn't it be nice to know with certainty that you are already living your ideal life?

WHAT IS THE POINT OF THE 'FIND YOUR LIFE PURPOSE' EXERCISE AGAIN?

Our entire lives are about creating meaning from what happens around us, so why not create a big picture vision that, well, means something to you? Isn't it a good idea to tap into what your life is really about instead of defaulting to any old meaning?

At the very least, the 15-minute purpose exercise will give you an insight into YOU. Taking a step back and tapping into what you like to do, what you are good at and what is important to you often brings out the best in people. It will show you where you can combine your passions, strengths and core values to shine in the world.

And don't worry; you really don't have to figure out something special or amazing. The template will direct you to create a purpose statement that is about being your best self and being nice to others. That is all.

What WOULD be special is if more people started living their lives in this way.

WHAT IF I WRITE OUT MY PURPOSE STATEMENT AND IT IS NOT 'RIGHT'?

It doesn't have to be perfect. What you come up with is better than the nothing you had before, true?

DO I REALLY HAVE TO FIGURE OUT THE PURPOSE OF MY LIFE?

No. You don't HAVE to find your purpose. As my coach says, the only thing you HAVE to do in life is breathe. Sit with that for a moment. You also don't have to watch a sunset, walk in a forest, eat chocolate, visit a museum or smell the roses. But it adds a richness and depth to your life that makes it worth living, so why wouldn't you? What have you got to lose? Especially if it only takes a few minutes.

Won't it take up too much time to get an answer?

No. Only 15 minutes. It's in the title of the book.

If I had a purpose wouldn't I just know it?

I am a pragmatic kind of girl and I like the thought of deciding on a purpose and directing my future, BUT I am also a romantic and I like the thought that life is magical and the universe may just have a plan for me. So which is it? Let's examine the arguments.

In the blue corner we have author and wise soul, Martha Beck, amongst others. They say that every human being has a divine purpose in life, a mission to fulfill, a path to follow. Our right lives whisper at us from our deepest selves. You may think you have no idea, but your soul knows why you are here. During idle times, when you dream or if you really lean into your intuition and listen, your true self tells you what your direction should be and what your destiny is.

Many people understand this at some level as they feel something is missing, that they are not fulfilling their destiny or contributing to the world in a way they know they can. Often it is because our daily lives cloud our 'North Star'—Martha's metaphor for our life purpose—and we need to find ways to make the night sky clear once again.

You are not 'deciding' on a purpose, but instead unearthing or rediscovering it. You already have it but want to bring it out into the open and in doing so become more of your essential core self: more YOU.

BUT—having to dig deep and uncover your perfect life purpose meant only for you—well, I hate to say it, but this is an awful lot of pressure. Also this seems to link into a notion of pre-destiny, which makes me feel a bit icky, like I don't have the freedom to choose. And it implies you have only one unchangeable purpose whereas I like to think you can find a general purpose and tweak it a bit as you progress through your life.

So what is the alternative?

In the red corner we have educator and chess master, Adam Robinson, amongst others. This is their point of view: you can simply decide on the type of person you want to become and how you want to live your life. Decide on it and then live it.

Your future is not pre-destined. It is based on what you are doing and thinking right now and so can be shaped. There is a choice in every moment. Take charge of your life and your future by taking charge of your present.

Stop searching for your purpose. Stop wasting time looking. Invent it. Find something meaningful and important to you and direct your life so you nurture it. Also know that you may not have one true calling, but a multitude of purposes as you grow and evolve to create an overall excellent life.

BUT—if you don't have an innate purpose or if you have many of them is it really a true mission? If it is not, then what is the point of finding it? This way at best seems not very magical and at worst seems a bit 'fake it till you make it' in style.

So, does it really matter? Whether you discover OR decide on your purpose may just be a difference in semantics. I have found 'find' sits relatively nicely in the middle of the two ways of looking at purpose. You may see the use of 'discover', 'uncover', 'create' or 'decide' instead of 'find'. It doesn't infer I agree with one viewpoint over the other.

Most people are happy to sit at the debate table rather than take the leap to find their purpose, as then they may have to get honest with themselves, vulnerable, and uncomfortable. They would rather argue all day long than take action on a purpose-driven life.

Either way, your dreams will remain dreams unless you find courage to achieve them. Divine inspiration is unlikely to smack you over the head, but regardless of what you believe, you are designed with the ability to determine the life you are meant to live.

Whether we already have a purpose deep inside of all of us, or we create it with our drive and action is beside the point. If you can't elucidate it, don't have it clearly in mind, then it is not helpful to you.

> You want your purpose to be front and center, not whispering at you from the sidelines.

Isn't it a lot of hard work, and for what?

First, I hope you can see by now that finding your purpose doesn't have to be hard work. So to answer the 'for what' piece—here are some benefits of knowing your purpose.

Personal development master, Tony Robbins, has popularized the theory that we all have six human needs. These are needs, not wants. We crave these on a deep level. One of the primary needs is a need for **certainty**—to feel safe and secure and to know that our expectations will be met.

Figuring out your purpose meets your need for certainty in a major way. It can simplify and clarify your life. It is a filter for action. A lighthouse that provides direction. It is a foundation to structure your life around. It assists with prioritizing your time around what is really important to you.

In tough times, purpose can give you an inner drive to continue. When times are easier it brings more energy and compassion into your life.

In the research—check out the Bluezones website—it is linked to a longer, happier life, which is statistically significant at a whopping seven years longer!

Other studies have linked knowing your purpose with better physical health (e.g.: better immunity, less likelihood of dementia), improved mental health (e.g.: lower rates of depression) and superior overall wellbeing (e.g.: better sleep, more friends).

According to big Tony, we have six needs, but only four of them—certainty, variety, significance and love—are met in everyone. The other two needs for growth and contribution are not always considered. Finding your purpose is a way to meet these two essential but sometimes neglected needs.

Purpose helps you to grow as it illuminates where you must move to in order to be your best self. This may be challenging, but ultimately any growth helps you to feel fulfilled.

Even more important, a purpose is not fully realized unless it has a transcendent part to it, a view on impacting, sharing or giving to others. When you are doing what you are meant to do, you benefit the world in an irreplaceable way. If you do not share your unique gifts and potentially help others, then you are doing a disservice to the world.

In short, finding your purpose assists you in meeting your very real need for contribution.

How you can use your new purpose to meet your essential needs for growth and contribution is discussed in the 'Supercharge Your Purpose' chapter.

Can my life purpose be changed?

Figuring out your purpose can be a once in a lifetime thing, or you can reflect on it each year or two and refine or tweak it. It should help you feel focused, not confined. You never do anything for your whole life, so why would your purpose be any different?

Does everyone have a purpose?

I think so, but it doesn't really matter what I think. What do you think? And do you really care? Isn't it more important to decide on your own purpose?

Do I have to change my life?

People get scared of change. But who you really are deep down is not changing. You are aligning more with your essential self. Some of your patterns and behaviors may change. How the external world reacts is what you are really worried about. We will talk in depth about how to deal with this later. But for now, get excited. After all, change is inevitable, the only constant in life is change, and now YOU are driving it.

What IS the point of it all?

It is easy to feel overwhelmed and insignificant. But the very fact that we live in a vast universe filled with mostly nothing and we are alive, here, right now is a miracle beyond miracles that is mind-bogglingly amazing.

> Don't think of the universe as nothingness. Think of it as limitless.

Sure, everyone dies, the end can come at any moment and death seems like a terrible and permanent conclusion. But death is what makes life profound. Our limited time here IS what is meaningful. Imagine how bored immortals like vampires would be!

Let's enjoy the journey instead of riding out the time until it is all over. We owe the gift of life our appreciation and action, not our disdain and lethargy. As cosmologist, Lawrence Krauss notes, even if the universe doesn't have a purpose, "We should not despair, but humbly rejoice in… our brief moment in the sun."

All of us have no idea what we are doing here on a fast spinning planet in the corner of a small galaxy on the edge of a vast universe, so we may as well play in the nonsense and absurdity and try to have a blast.

Don't fight it. Live in the ridiculous.

We are currently alive in the most safe and abundant time in human history, on a planet thriving with life, with a sun that shines, fresh water that pours out of the sky, and sometimes when the combination of the two is just right, we get rainbows.

As Jen Sincero says in her fabulous book, *You are a Badass*: "The fact that we aren't stumbling around in a state of awe is appalling."

We have now smashed through your main objections to finding your purpose, and you should be absolutely pumped and ready to find your purpose in 15 minutes in the next chapter.

Purpose Statements

Grace: *The purpose of my life is to be fulfilled, healthy, and fun, so that I can share my sincere and grateful self with the world.*

Vartika: *The purpose of my life is to be happy, to have fun, and to contribute to the community as well as to inspire others.*

Jackie: *The purpose of my life is to be living, happy, healthy, fun, to grow and be compassionate to make a difference and gift to others.*

Catherine: *The purpose of my life is to solve challenging health problems to enable people to move forward with their lives.*

WHAT ARE YOUR OBJECTIONS TO FINDING YOUR PURPOSE?

Write down the objections from above that resonate most with you. Add in any further objections you may have. What answers to your objections are the most helpful so you can get on with discovering, writing down and taking action on your life's purpose?

5
FIND YOUR PURPOSE IN 15 MINUTES

 'Every day, think as you wake up, today I am fortunate to be alive, I have a precious human life, I am not going to waste it.' – Dalai Lama

ONE LAST OBJECTION

You may be thinking "How can this be my real purpose if it doesn't take a lot of time and work?" The fact that it takes 15 minutes doesn't make it any less real. Plucking the words from a list doesn't make it any less relevant. And using a template as a kind of 'paint by numbers' purpose statement doesn't make it any less original or unique to you.

One of the early volunteers said:

> "I really loved this! I was shocked to have broken my perception that finding my purpose had to be difficult and time consuming – thank you!"

Chapter Note

This chapter will have plenty of questions, prompts and lines for each section of the exercise so that you start drafting your purpose statement. At the end of the chapter, there will be a repeat of the Find Your Purpose in 15 Minutes *exercise so that you can further refine your purpose.*

How excited are you on a scale from 1 to 10?

_____

_____

_____

Purpose Recap

Your purpose is your WHY for being here. It is what you live for, what is important to you and what makes your life significant and worthwhile. Don't worry if you find your purpose and your life looks nothing like it! You can start to use it as a guiding light, something to aspire to.

A purpose statement should be short, positive and powerfully resonate with you.

The template below is a useful foundation that can also be rearranged to fit your unique purpose statement.

> **Definition:** Your purpose is about who you want to BE and what you want to DO so that you have an IMPACT on others.
>
> **Template:** 'The purpose of my life is to (be and/or do) _____ to (impact) _____.'

Purpose Examples

E.g.: The purpose of my life is to be courageous, abundance-oriented and full of gratitude so that I can share my gifts with others and help the environment.

E.g.: The purpose of my life is to be loving, joyful and healthy so that I can learn, grow and create and then encourage others to success.

E.g.: The purpose of my life is to be full of passion so I can use my determination and inquisitive nature to help to make a difference in my community and the world.

The Fab List

One of the most difficult parts of finding your purpose is coming up with the right words to use.

Here is where the 15-minute purpose exercise makes things super easy for you.

It gives you all the words you need!

It simply hands them out on a silver platter.

First is '**The Fab List**' – a selection of 20 positive words along with their associated words and short phrases.

Simply look over these 100+ tasty bites and choose your favorites to use in the your 'BE' and 'DO' elements in the first part of the purpose statement.

- Love – nice, kind, caring, grace
- Healthy – energy, vitality, wellbeing, fit, strong
- Happy – joy, cheerful, positive, optimistic, fulfilled
- Fun – enjoy, playful, humor, laughter
- Grow – learn, discover, improve, master, knowledge
- Achieve – accomplish, success, excellence, live my dreams

- Create – imagine, innovate, invent, art
- Courage – brave, confident, bold, adventurous, face fear
- Passionate – excitement, enthusiastic, zest for life
- Give – help, contribute, serve, generous, benevolent
- Peace – calm, simplicity, tranquil, serene, rest
- Curious – inquisitive, interested, wonder, be in awe
- Spiritual – aware, conscious, wholeness, mindful, transcendent
- Integrity – fair, honest, sincere, true, open
- Authentic – real, genuine, be me, be myself, be true to me
- Ideal self – be my best self, reach my potential, be a good person
- Appreciate – gratitude, grateful, thankful, treasure
- Compassionate – supportive, considerate, empathetic, thoughtful, warm
- Persistent – determined, driven, motivated, ambitious, grit
- Abundance – wealth, freedom, beauty, wisdom, power

The Impact Lists

The two '**Impact Lists**' are then used to complete the second half of the purpose statement about your impact on others.

There are verbs such as 'give', 'work towards' and 'inspire' and then nouns such as 'others', 'my community' and 'the world' to select from.

Verbs

- Give – help, gift, provide, give abundance to
- Share – serve, share my gifts, contribute, nourish, delight
- Connect – teach, write, speak, learn, read
- Lead – empower, inspire, encourage, spread magic, focus on
- Accept – listen, understand, heal, forgive
- Make a difference – give hope to, work towards, stand for, challenge

Nouns

- Non-specific – others, humans, all beings, people, creatures
- Specific – organizations, causes, charities, community, groups
- Friends and Family – loved ones, my family, my children, my tribe
- General – the world, the environment, nature, my legacy

Word Lists Housekeeping

Use any of the words. They are displayed in a manner that is meant to make them easier to read and choose, not because the 'main' word is more important than the associated words and phrases.

Feel free to highlight all the words you like. Then try and narrow down to the most important ones for you.

It is okay to drop a few of the words when writing out your purpose statement. They won't mind.

You may need to change the words slightly to fit into your purpose statement ('love' to 'loving', 'create' to 'creative', 'power' to 'powerful', etc.).

If you have a word not in the lists that best suits your purpose, please use it.

People say these lists nudge them to come up with other words, or they add a faith-based component as well.

Find Your Purpose in 15 Minutes Instructions

1. Take a deep breath and say in an excited voice: 'I will find my purpose today!'

Write out 'I will find my purpose today!'

_____

_____

_____

2. Keep this purpose statement template in mind:

'The purpose of my life is to (be and/or do) _____ to (impact) _____'

Purpose Statement Template

The purpose of my life is to be / do…

_____

_____

…to (impact)

_____

_____

3. READ THE FAB LIST BELOW AND HIGHLIGHT OR WRITE DOWN ANY words that resonate the most with you. Most people eventually settle on between 2 and 8 words:

- Love – nice, kind, caring, grace
- Healthy – energy, vitality, wellbeing, fit, strong
- Happy – joy, cheerful, positive, optimistic, fulfilled
- Fun – enjoy, playful, humor, laughter
- Grow – learn, discover, improve, master, knowledge
- Achieve – accomplish, success, excellence, live my dreams
- Create – imagine, innovate, invent, art
- Courage – brave, confident, bold, adventurous, face fear
- Passionate – excitement, enthusiastic, zest for life
- Give – help, contribute, serve, generous, benevolent
- Peace – calm, simplicity, tranquil, serene, rest
- Curious – inquisitive, interested, wonder, be in awe
- Spiritual – aware, conscious, wholeness, mindful, transcendent
- Integrity – fair, honest, sincere, true, open
- Authentic – real, genuine, be me, be myself, be true to me
- Ideal self – be my best self, reach my potential, be a good person
- Appreciate – gratitude, grateful, thankful, treasure
- Compassionate – supportive, considerate, empathetic, thoughtful, warm
- Persistent – determined, driven, motivated, ambitious, grit
- Abundance – wealth, freedom, beauty, wisdom, power

FAVORITE WORDS FROM THE FAB LIST

Write out the words from The Fab List *that resonate most with you and add in any of your own.*

_____

_____

_____

_____

_____

_____

4. Read the **Impact Lists** below and highlight or write down the verbs and nouns that fit the impact part of your purpose statement. Most people choose between 1 and 3 words from each list:

Verbs

- Give – help, gift, provide, give abundance to
- Share – serve, share my gifts, contribute, nourish, delight
- Connect – teach, write, speak, learn, read
- Lead – empower, inspire, encourage, spread magic, focus on
- Accept – listen, understand, heal, forgive
- Make a difference – give hope to, work towards, stand for, challenge

Nouns

- Non-specific – others, humans, all beings, people, creatures
- Specific – organizations, causes, charities, community, groups
- Friends and Family – loved ones, my family, my children, my tribe
- General – the world, the environment, nature, my legacy

FAVORITE WORDS FROM THE IMPACT LISTS

Write out the words from the Impact Lists *that fit the impact part of your purpose statement and add in any of your own.*

_____

_____

_____

_____

_____

_____

_____

5. Take out a pen and paper and write out

    'The purpose of my life is to ____'

MY PURPOSE STATEMENT (DRAFTS)

The purpose of my life is to

_____

_____

_____

6. Add your favorite words from **The Fab List** and the **Impact Lists** into the template and rewrite your purpose statement until it powerfully resonates with you.

This may take a handful of attempts but you WILL get there.

MY PURPOSE STATEMENT (REWRITES)

The purpose of my life is to

7. Read your final purpose statement aloud.

MY PURPOSE STATEMENT (FINAL)

The purpose of my life is to

_____

_____

_____

_____

Congratulations, just like that you have found your purpose!

IS IT GOOD ENOUGH?

You have a purpose statement but you are not sure if it is 'good enough'. Use this quick checklist to find out. A purpose statement should be:

- short (one or two sentences)
- positive (makes you very happy)
- easy to experience (every single day)
- powerfully resonate with you (just feels right)

If you are not sure if it is quite right yet, put it aside for today, look at it with fresh eyes tomorrow and tweak it if needed.

Maybe you still think your purpose statement is not 'good enough' as it was such a quick and simple exercise. This is what some of the early volunteers had to say:

"I hadn't ever thought to do this in writing before, but this made it so easy; it's focused my mind and heart and I'm glad to see that my purpose statement is actually true to my life now and shows so much growth potential."

"This is very insightful and I wish I had done it a long time ago. It's comforting and liberating at the same time. It makes all the noise fall away and gives that clarity we are always looking to find."

"Thank you for giving me some of my drive back that I have been struggling with."

"I love my purpose statement. It really resonates with me and I use it every day. Thank you."

PLEASE, if you haven't done the 15-minute purpose exercise yet, give it a go.

Wear It In

Your purpose statement may feel a little tight, a bit scratchy. The next chapter explains how to ingrain your purpose statement so it becomes comfortably part of you. The following chapter gives you some tips on how to really live your purpose, even if your life looks nothing like your purpose statement.

Stick around. Finding your purpose in 15 minutes is just the beginning.

Purpose Statements

Jodi: *The purpose of my life is to be authentic and to live my truth so others will be inspired to do the same.*

Cill: *The purpose of my life is to encourage bravery and compassion by being courageous and caring to all the people I am in contact with.*

Nicole: *The purpose of my life is to create and nourish loving relationships so that I can live a life full of love and fulfillment and hopefully inspire others to do the same and succeed in their world.*

Georgie: *The purpose of my life is to be conscious in reaching my full potential through living a life full of love, happiness, compassion, joy, knowledge, abundance and gratitude by being open and mastering my true self; so that I can be creative, teach, empower, inspire, help and heal others and the earth by sharing my love, wisdom and gifts.*

Find Your Purpose in 15 Minutes Instructions

1. Write out 'I will find my purpose today!'

_____

_____

_____

_____

2. Purpose Statement Template

The purpose of my life is to be / do…

_____

_____

_____

_____

…to (impact)

_____

_____

_____

_____

3. Favorite Words from The Fab List

Write out the 2 to 8 words from The Fab List *that resonate most with you and add in any of your own.*

- Love – nice, kind, caring, grace
- Healthy – energy, vitality, wellbeing, fit, strong
- Happy – joy, cheerful, positive, optimistic, fulfilled
- Fun – enjoy, playful, humor, laughter
- Grow – learn, discover, improve, master, knowledge
- Achieve – accomplish, success, excellence, live my dreams
- Create – imagine, innovate, invent, art
- Courage – brave, confident, bold, adventurous, face fear
- Passionate – excitement, enthusiastic, zest for life
- Give – help, contribute, serve, generous, benevolent
- Peace – calm, simplicity, tranquil, serene, rest
- Curious – inquisitive, interested, wonder, be in awe
- Spiritual – aware, conscious, wholeness, mindful, transcendent
- Integrity – fair, honest, sincere, true, open
- Authentic – real, genuine, be me, be myself, be true to me
- Ideal self – be my best self, reach my potential, be a good person
- Appreciate – gratitude, grateful, thankful, treasure
- Compassionate – supportive, considerate, empathetic, thoughtful, warm
- Persistent – determined, driven, motivated, ambitious, grit
- Abundance – wealth, freedom, beauty, wisdom, power

_____

_____

_____

_____

_____

_____

_____

_____

_____

4. Favorite Words from the Impact Lists

Write out the 1 to 3 words from each of the Impact Lists *that fit the impact part of your purpose statement and add in any of your own.*

Verbs

- Give – help, gift, provide, give abundance to
- Share – serve, share my gifts, contribute, nourish, delight
- Connect – teach, write, speak, learn, read
- Lead – empower, inspire, encourage, spread magic, focus on
- Accept – listen, understand, heal, forgive
- Make a difference – give hope to, work towards, stand for, challenge

Nouns

- Non-specific – others, humans, all beings, people, creatures
- Specific – organizations, causes, charities, community, groups
- Friends and Family – loved ones, my family, my children, my tribe
- General – the world, the environment, nature, my legacy

5. My Purpose Statement (Drafts)

The purpose of my life is to

6. My Purpose Statement (Rewrites)

The purpose of my life is to

_____

_____

_____

_____

_____

_____

7. My Purpose Statement (Final)

The purpose of my life is to

_____

_____

_____

_____

Congratulations, just like that you have found your purpose!

6

PLANT YOUR PURPOSE IN YOUR MIND, HEART AND SOUL

 'Life is either a daring adventure or nothing at all.' – Helen Keller

CROSS IT OFF THE LIST

Wow, just like that you have your purpose statement! You have a simple way to think about and express your life purpose. You can check 'find the purpose of your life' off your to-do list!

So what do you do now?

There are three simple steps that will take you from finding your purpose to thoroughly enfolding it into your life. The steps are:

1. Read, display and review your purpose so it is ingrained in your mind
2. Link practices around it such as incantations, visualizations, empowering questions or a gratitude ritual so it is embedded in your heart

3. Find ways to use it as a filter and a guide every day in the real world so it is part of the core YOU, in your soul

Let's go over each of these steps in more detail…

1. Plant Your Purpose in Your Mind

Make sure that you have your purpose statement somewhere you have easy access to it and see it every day. Use a pen and paper version or print it out and stick it to your wall, on the fridge or on the bathroom mirror. For those who are more private, put it inside the door to your wardrobe or tuck it into a journal you write in regularly.

If you have an electronic document of your purpose, place that document on your computer desktop, or add it into your notes app or books app on your phone so you can open it up and read it regularly.

Some of you may want to share your newfound purpose on your favorite social media feed, on Pinterest or on your own blog. Sharing it with others keeps you accountable to live your life on purpose, but it does have a potential downside in that some people may be less than enthusiastic about it.

A fun and completely optional way to display your purpose statement is to create a 'vision board' of it. A vision board is any sort of board on which you display images that represent items that can relate to your purpose—images of role models you want to be like, what you want to do and create in your lifetime and who you want to help or share your gifts with. Create one the old-fashioned way out of cutouts from magazines stuck to a big piece of paper or cardboard. Or combine some pictures into an online board on Pinterest or elsewhere.

An extra cool idea is to take a photo of your written purpose statement or its physical vision board and upload it so it becomes your computer screen saver or wallpaper on your phone. We look at our phones on average over 100 times a day (yes really!), so your purpose statement will be reviewed, at least subconsciously, an enormous amount.

These ideas help you remember and easily recite your purpose statement. At this point I usually get asked what to do if you want to change your purpose. If it seems fine to you, then please don't amend it unless it is a tweak as a result of the extra introspection (navel-gazing) chapters coming up next. Leave it for at least six months, and then use the tools above to read and remember a revised version after that point.

2. Plant Your Purpose in Your Heart

Displaying and reading your purpose statement on a repeated basis gives you a cognitive level of understanding it. You will know your purpose inside out and back to front. But for it to really stick, you need to feel like it is part of you. It needs to connect with your emotional center, your heart.

There are a number of ways to do this, so select one or two and try them out. Some of them can also be mixed together to make a mega-tool. Yes, they may seem a bit strange, but they are also a bit of fun, so why not give them a go?

Affirmations and Incantations

Affirmations and incantations are long words that basically mean saying your purpose statement (or anything else) aloud, often and in a repeated fashion. Affirmations are associated with saying things in the mirror. Incantations are not usually in front of a mirror but have more power and emotion behind them. They are often done standing in a strong posture and speaking with a loud, confident voice. You can feel a little silly about it, but they are a great, no-cost way of embedding in your purpose statement. Plus they don't have to take up any extra time—do them while putting on your makeup or shaving, driving in your car or as part of your morning exercise and mindset routine.

Empowering Questions

If you don't feel like you are quite up to affirmations and incantations, what can you do instead? Well just like the start of this paragraph, you can use questions in a more effective way. Using empowering questions has been found to have a greater impact on outcomes than affirmations because if a question is asked, even if it is not spoken aloud, your mind is still compelled to answer it. So ask yourself (silently or out loud) questions such as:

> 'How can I live my purpose even more?', or
> 'What is one thing I can do today to help me be more on purpose?' or
> 'What would the person I want to become do right now?'

Then listen to your heart's response.

Visualization

For the visual people or dreamers out there, there is a less noisy way of connecting deeply with your purpose. Take a few moments of alone time, get comfortable, close your eyes and imagine what your life would be like with your purpose fully realized. Create the most vivid and descriptive mental picture as you can. Invoke your senses: what would you be doing, seeing, smelling, feeling? Please try not to think about the 'how' of what you have just conjured up. Simply bask in the warm glow of your purpose-fuelled life visualization for a few moments.

GRATITUDE RITUAL

Being grateful creates awareness of the good in your life. Gratitude studies have shown that an appreciation practice is associated with being more enthusiastic about life, being interested in the community, being kinder to others and getting better sleep, among a myriad of other positive outcomes. Be thankful for knowing you can easily find your purpose. Feel appreciative when you think of living your life on purpose. And feel gratitude in combination with any of the above techniques. It works especially well as part of the visualization exercise.

3. PLANT YOUR PURPOSE IN YOUR SOUL

You may now be thinking that all this reciting of my purpose sounds great, BUT my life looks NOTHING like the purpose I wrote down! For some people this will be exciting and for others this will be downright scary. Now that you know your purpose there is no denying or ignoring it any longer, and this can be a challenging place to be.

The next chapter will go into more depth on how to live with purpose including tackling some of the major issues that can come up when you start to live with a mission in life. It will give you some tips on what to do to change your life so it starts to fit around your newfound purpose, how to get back in alignment when you derail from your purpose and what to do about the naysayers.

For now, here is the BEST tip to start living your life with your purpose front and center. Are you ready? Drum roll please...

SAY 'NO'.

Your purpose will mean some things need to be shed from your life. You need to remove the good to make way for the great. Putting boundaries around your purposeful life will feel right but will be difficult, at least at first. If you do not learn to say 'no', then you are saying 'YES' to someone else's agenda and 'NO' to yourself.

You can still be a lovely person and say no. Author, researcher and TED speaker, Brené Brown says: "Compassionate people ask for what they need. They say no when they need to, and when they say yes, they mean it. They're compassionate because their boundaries keep them out of resentment."

Even in the nicest way possible, saying 'no' is uncomfortable, so practice on small things and build up. Here are a few ways to say 'no' politely:

- "Sounds wonderful, but that is not part of my work focus right now."
- "Sorry but my current commitments mean I cannot take that on."
- "It sounds amazing but I wouldn't be able to give that the attention it deserves."
- "I can't help you right now but I can schedule it after X date."
- "Sorry it is not my policy to do X." (People respect policies, even ones you have made up yourself!)

If a 'no' is done well, people should be happy with how clear you are and how committed you are to what is important to you. And if they are not happy? Well, their response is their problem. We will talk more about dealing with the critics in the next chapter.

Keep Climbing

It may sound too easy to be true, but repeating your newfound purpose over and over WILL mean that you start to truly believe and embody your purpose. But we can't just live inside our heads and our hearts. We must start manifesting what our purpose is directing us to do.

Finding your purpose is your first stage. Believing it is the second. Living it is the third. Take it one rung at a time but keep moving up.

HOW ARE YOU GOING TO PLANT YOUR PURPOSE IN YOUR LIFE?

Write down the ideas from above that resonate most with you. Add in any further ideas to plant your purpose in your mind, heart and soul.

_____

_____

_____

_____

_____

_____

_____

_____

_____

_____

_____

Purpose Statements

Nikita: *The purpose of my life is to be happy and peaceful so that I can connect and share delight with loved ones and the world.*

Sally: *The purpose of my life is to be constantly learning and writing so that I can help women everywhere share their unique gifts and create a life they love.*

Carole: *The purpose of my life is to be a good person, kind, successful, compassionate and living honestly and with integrity so that I can give generously, abundantly and with love to my tribe and to causes I believe in.*

Richard: *The purpose of my life is to be empathetic, to be curious to learn and challenge myself and create, to enable me to be content, supportive to people I care about, to have patience with myself and family and be there for my son as he grows.*

My Purpose Statement

The purpose of my life is to

_____

_____

_____

_____

7
PURPOSE IN THE REAL WORLD

 'And the day came when the risk to remain tight in a bud was more painful than the risk it took to blossom.' – Anais Nin

The 'N' Issues

You now have a purpose and you are trying hard to get it ingrained in your mind, heart and soul with the techniques from the last chapter, but you still might not be so sure exactly how to really LIVE it.

People who find their purpose end up in a few different categories. This chapter addresses your burning questions depending on where you have landed with your purpose.

Here are three main issues to acquiring a new purpose:

- The Non-believers: "I have found a purpose, but my life looks nothing like it. I don't truly believe I can live it, and I am not sure where to even begin."
- The Neglecters: "I have found a purpose, and it mostly matches my life already, so I am thrilled, but I can fall out of alignment with it and am not sure how to get back on track."
- The Naysayers: "I have found a purpose, I love it and I am embarking on making a few changes in my life, but now I am experiencing some negative reactions from other people."

Help for the Non-believers

You have glimpsed your ultimate purpose, and now your mind is telling you that it is not possible to have a life that embraces it. This is a common but cruel reaction to finding your purpose. I understand wanting to hide from it. There is a lot of fear associated with purpose—fear of success, fear of failure, fear of what others may think.

Congratulations! Give yourself a pat on the back as you have overcome some of your fear to find your purpose. Most people don't even get that far. Now you have to fight your mind gremlins to really believe in it and start living it.

With curiosity and not judgment, look at the negative beliefs and limiting stories that your mind is telling you. Uncover what is behind you not allowing yourself to live your best life. Your thoughts are only thoughts; they are not necessarily true. What would happen if you just stopped believing that notion and started believed something that permitted you to live a life of purpose?

There is a ton more that can be said here, but please don't let some old story you have told yourself stop you from living the life you are supposed to live. Check out my book, *Crappy to Happy*, if all this piques your interest.

What do you do if you want to change your life but don't know where to start? Start doing something. Anything at all. You have now tapped into some of your passions, strengths and values. Take action on one of them. Choose an activity, hobby, side-hustle idea or problem in the world you would like to fix and start working on it. Take a class, find a mentor, join a team, create something. Start small and see where it leads. And if it doesn't work, try something else. Fail forward.

People think belief has to come before action, but often you can direct your behavior towards something and that changes your thinking about it. You are not going to be good at writing / dancing / engineering overnight, but by learning and practicing you develop these into strengths and passions that confirm your purpose. Clarity comes from taking action.

As blogger and potty mouth, Mark Mansen states: "Life is about not knowing and then doing something anyway. All of life is like this. It never changes."

Purpose is only a concept until you pick a direction and start to learn and master some skills. You can't share your gifts with the world until you have put some genuine effort into trying things that you think you may enjoy and want to share. Think of it as growing into your purpose. Everyone knows growing up does not happen overnight.

Non-believer Issue

Do you think you have a non-believer issue? How might you minimize or overcome this issue? What mindset changes or actions could help? List them here.

_____

_____

_____

_____

_____

_____

_____

_____

Help for the Neglecters

You found your purpose earlier and realized that you have been living it all along. Your purpose statement fits like a glove over your existing life. You feel like you are already mostly living your purpose. Congratulations, you are one lucky human.

The main issue you may have is sometimes forgetting about or neglecting your purpose. You stray off the track of your purpose-driven life and need to be guided back. First, don't beat yourself up as no one lives his or her life entirely on purpose all the time. Be kind to yourself. You have permission to not write the next book or build your socially conscious business and instead scroll, binge watch or get to the next game level.

Simply remember to check in now and again between the different areas of your life—relationships, work, health etc.—and see if you are mostly living your purpose.

> If you fall out of alignment, pull yourself back in with grace and without judgment.

What you can do to align with your purpose doesn't have to be extraordinary. Spend time with your kids without your phone, pay someone a compliment or give yourself an hour to go for a run, read a book or paint a picture. Reread your purpose statement, do exercises like incantations to get your purpose ingrained, and wake up to a new day with your purpose woven even more into the fabric of your life.

Neglecter Issue

Do you think you have a neglecter issue? How might you minimize or overcome this issue? What mindset changes or actions could help? List them here.

_____

_____

_____

_____

_____

_____

_____

Dealing with the Naysayers

The two above issues are mostly within your control to solve. You decide what to believe, how to take action and when to pull your life back in line with your purpose.

What can you do if something is outside your immediate control? What do you do if you have a negative reaction from others?

First, check whether there really is an undesirable, external response to you living your purpose. Often people have a mindset that everybody won't like the new you or that 'people' will be upset if you change your life. Most of this is just garbage spewing out from your mind gremlins and does not reflect your reality. If there is no actual discouraging reaction but you still think there is, then you need to do some work on your limiting beliefs—question them and cut them out if they don't serve you.

Second, you can change your life subtly. Move incrementally towards your purpose. You don't have to tell anyone. You can decide to be more cheerful at home, write a book on the train to work or save a few dollars each week to visit that place in the world you have always dreamed of seeing. Honestly, most people won't notice. You will have a lighter feeling and you will know you have put in the work to create it, but others, even close loved ones, will continue on like normal.

Last, yes, sometimes, there is an actual proper attack on the new you, which, remember, is really the core you. Occasionally naysayers try to sabotage you working towards your purpose. First, unless they are close to you, don't pay them any notice. So what if the media or the culture doesn't like it? But if they are connected to you in some way—family, close friends, colleagues—then you may have to deal with it.

If there is a comment or even friction from your family, explain that you are working on becoming nicer and happier for them. Shift the focus back to them. Tell them you are going to be the same person but more YOU: less distracted, less stressed, happier and more fun. How could anyone say they wouldn't like that? Plus they are your family; they should want the best for you. If friends or colleagues are questioning you, then use this tool from author and wise soul, Martha Beck: practice saying this simple phrase to any naysayer:

> "All is well."

If there is still some conflict, realize that their reactions are just coming from their own needs, and you have the power to respond in the most resourceful way you can. Repeat that this is how things will be, be gracious when interacting with them and limit your time with the naysayers to what is absolutely necessary. Then go and find a tribe that understands and respects your new, beautiful, authentic way of living. They are out there waiting for you.

Naysayer Issue

Do you think you have a naysayer issue? How might you minimize or overcome this issue? What mindset changes or actions could help? List them here.

_____

_____

_____

_____

_____

_____

_____

Living on Purpose

You have taken steps to make your life match your purpose, but how do you really know you are living it? It may feel good, but it may not. New challenges arise and sometimes life can seem harder than it once was. You could take that as a sign that you are not living your real purpose or living it in the right way.

Many people say they notice that even though there will be issues and stumbles, overall they feel more energized, confident and free. How do you feel in general now that you have defined your purpose?

I know my purpose is shining through when there is some unexpected benefit or strange coincidence that arises from my new way of living. Since becoming an author, through a series of small-world connections, I managed to get back in touch with a friend with whom I lost contact with over ten years ago. I was also gifted a crystal bracelet from another friend who credits me with partly inspiring her to start her own side business. These are not outcomes I could have possibly directed or foreseen, but these ripple effects make me feel like my purpose-driven life is on the right track.

Now that your purpose is clear to you, your life WILL change. This is a scary concept—no one loves change—but you can navigate this with acceptance and grace.

So whether you decide to take a big leap or let your newfound purpose guide you into incremental shifts, welcome to your new life.

Navel-gazing

Many of the early volunteers for the find your purpose in 15-minute exercise loved being given the chance for a bit of introspection and reflection.

There were comments like:

"I liked how it made me reflect on my life, loved it, thank you."

"I can feel confident that I've reviewed all areas of my life, my priorities and my inner desires."

"This reflection was a great start to my day!"

"It pushed me out of my comfort zone. As a typical man this makes you think about feelings and what you want from life which does get a little bit deep for a Tuesday lunchtime but it's always good to check your direction."

The next three chapters are for those of you, like these early volunteers, who really enjoyed the short exercise in finding your purpose and want some more of that juicy goodness.

- Chapter Eight suggests personality and psychological tests you can take to find out more about yourself.
- Chapter Nine gives a variety of questions to ponder.
- Chapter Ten provides some exercises that give you a deeper grasp of who you are, what you are here for and the legacy you want to leave behind.

These three chapters are entirely optional and you can skip them if you like, but they may help cement in that purpose statement a little more, so why not take a little journey through them?

Purpose Statements

Gael: *The purpose of my life is to love and give to inspire others.*

Courtney: *The purpose of my life is to be creative, courageous and passionate so I can write fiction to impact others by bringing them escape, entertainment and joy.*

Sasha: *The purpose of my life is to be authentic, compassionate and warm so that I can inspire, encourage and help people to be confidently and courageously themselves, actively living in the life they love.*

Karen: *The purpose of my life is to be passionate about what I do, be courageous when I feel fear, be authentic to myself, appreciate all that I have, relish the small joys, be generous with my knowledge, skills and time, be compassionate and kind to others and finally be mindful of my impact on the environment.*

MY PURPOSE STATEMENT

The purpose of my life is to

_____

_____

_____

_____

8
DIVING DEEPER: TESTS

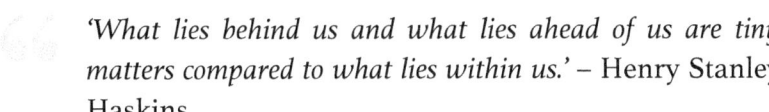
'What lies behind us and what lies ahead of us are tiny matters compared to what lies within us.' – Henry Stanley Haskins

LET'S GO DEEP

The next three chapters are:

- Tests – personality and values quizzes that reveal your characteristics
- Questions – queries that require thought-provoking answers about yourself
- Exercises – tasks that take a little more time to prompt insightful understanding of your inner workings

The tests are meant to be a bit of fun, to ease you into more of the navel-gazing work. The questions will challenge you to be truthful about the real you, and the exercises are designed to extract invaluable knowledge of your true self.

You can do these tests, questions and exercises split up over the course of a week or so or clear two hours and do them all at once.

I know I said 15 minutes, but what is a couple of hours in your long, long life?

You can skip the next three chapters, but here is why you may want to spend some of your valuable time reading them and then doing the tasks:

- You will get a deeper understanding of yourself in an overall sense.
- It will give you patterns and insights into your highest passions, values and strengths, which can help with day-to-day decisions and goal setting.
- With the above insights, you may revisit your purpose statement and tweak it to make it even more meaningful to you.
- The additional information gathered may help you supercharge your purpose with the tools detailed in Chapter Eleven.

The more you know about who you truly are, what motivates you, what you love to do and are great at, the clearer it will be to live a life of fulfillment and success.

Get in State

First, please get into the right physical and mental state for this. Before doing any of these tasks:

- take three deep belly breaths
- scrunch your shoulders up to your ears tight and then release
- shake your whole body out
- put a smile on your face

Now pretend you are meeting YOU for the first time. You are open and ready to find out things. You are relaxed but also up for a challenge.

Make sure you have something to write, tap or type your answers on.

You are good to go.

TEST PROS AND CONS

There are many tests that look at people's personalities, characteristics and drivers. Each of them will give you some insight into yourself, but they also come with limitations.

People worry the test will put them 'in a box' and define them according to archetypes that don't reflect the complex human they are. Conversely, people sometimes find that their results change over time or in a different mood or setting.

Overall, there is a question of how valid the test results can be.

Still, sometimes tests tell you things about yourself or give you an insight or show you a pattern that you had never put together before.

Aren't you just a little curious what the tests will highlight? Think of the results of the test as one tool in your toolbox, and combine it with the answers to the questions and the exercises to form a complete view of your essential self.

Test Housekeeping

With all tests, it is suggested to carefully read your individual result and notice words and phrases that come up repeatedly. Then check if these relate to your purpose.

Can your purpose be tweaked to incorporate these frequently used expressions that describe you?

You may find it is difficult to choose an answer to the test, so go with your gut or initial response.

Note that the websites may change or not be there at all. Some of the tests are free; some are no cost but require name and email details, and some of them require a payment. Whether a fee is charged and how much it is may be updated after this book is published as well.

All the following tests took between five and twenty minutes to do.

Myers-Briggs Type Indicator (MBTI) Personality Test

What is it?

From mbtionline.com: "Myers-Briggs…is designed to help you identify your preferred way of doing things in four key areas: directing and receiving energy, taking in information, making decisions, and approaching the outside world. Your natural preferences in these four areas sort into one of 16 distinct patterns of behavior called personality types."

What do the results look like?

You will end up with one of the 16 four-letter results that show your personality type, e.g.: ISTP or ENFJ.

Why do it?

From mbtionline.com: "The assessment gives you a framework for understanding yourself and appreciating differences in others."

What has it got to do with finding my purpose?

This gives an overall—and scarily accurate—picture of you and your preferences. It will help you determine whether your purpose statement fits with your personality type.

Where to do the test

At mbtionline.com the test is currently US$50.

At 16personalities.com the test is free as of the writing of this book.

Test Results - Myers-Briggs Type Indicator (MBTI)

_____

_____

_____

_____

_____

_____

_____

_____

Kolbe A Index

What is it?

From kolbe.com: "[An] assessment identifying the natural way that people take action. Left to our own choice, each of us has an instinctive way of problem solving. Research shows that people are most productive when they are free to choose their own method of accomplishing a task or providing a solution."

What do the results look like?

You will show preference in one or two of the four 'action modes': fact finder, follow through, quick start and implementer.

Why do it?

From kolbe.com: "People who've taken the Kolbe Indexes have become more confident, more energetic, and more powerful - just from understanding their natural talents. Kolbe focuses on what's right with you and tells you how to build on it. Kolbe doesn't just help you achieve your goals; it helps you control your destiny."

What has it got to do with finding my purpose?

This test shows you your natural strengths used in creative problem solving. It will tap into how you can be the best version of you, exactly what your purpose is aiming for.

Where to do the test

At kolbe.com the test is currently US$50.

Unfortunately there is no free version that is similar, but I highly recommend investing in this test.

TEST RESULTS - KOLBE A INDEX

_____

_____

_____

_____

_____

_____

THE FOUR TENDENCIES QUIZ

WHAT IS IT?

This short quiz, developed by author Gretchen Rubin, gives insight into how we respond to inner and outer expectations. It effectively answers how to get people—including ourselves—to do what we want.

WHAT DO THE RESULTS LOOK LIKE?

Most people show strong preference in one of four tendencies: upholder, questioner, obliger or rebel.

Why do it?

From quiz.gretchenrubin.com: "Knowing our Tendency can help us set up situations in the ways that make it more likely that we'll achieve our aims. We can make better decisions, meet deadlines, meet our promises to ourselves, suffer less stress, and engage more deeply with others."

What has it got to do with finding my purpose?

It can help to decide how you would be best suited to impact others. For example, an upholder could inspire others with their methods to commit to expectations. A questioner could use their questioning skills to evoke change in an area that they feel strongly about.

Where to do the test

At quiz.gretchenrubin.com the test is free as of the writing of this book.

Test Results - The Four Tendencies

_____

_____

_____

_____

_____

The 5 Love Languages Profile

What is it?

Author and marriage counselor, Gary Chapman, states that there are five love languages—different ways we prefer to give and receive love.

What do the results look like?

You will determine one or two primary love languages from the five types: words of affirmation, acts of service, receiving gifts, quality time and physical touch.

Why do it?

Discovering your primary love language will improve your connection to others.

What has it got to do with finding my purpose?

This test will help with your contribution part of purpose as it can show the best way you like to give. For instance, if you like words, then maybe you share your gifts through writing. If you prefer physical touch, you may decide to learn massage. If acts of service are most important, you may find yourself building schools in developing countries.

Where to do the test

At 5lovelanguages.com the test is free as of the writing of this book.

TEST RESULTS - THE 5 LOVE LANGUAGES

_____

_____

_____

_____

_____

_____

TESTS ABOUT STRENGTHS, PASSIONS AND VALUES

WHAT ARE THEY?

The Fab List comes from an in-depth look at all the best strengths, passions and values that relate to the meaning of life. The tests below pull out these words and phrases in an order that relates to you personally.

WHY DO THEM?

During the 15-minute purpose exercise, you simply chose from The Fab List and The Impact Lists the words and phrases that are most important to you. The tests below will confirm whether the words that resonated with you during the 15-minute exercise are your highest-ranking strengths, passions and values.

There are many benefits. Even if you don't achieve your purpose, your life will be better for knowing and pursuing your passions. Positive psychology research confirms that using your strengths to work towards something creates a more meaningful and happy life. Knowing your values enables you to make space for what is most important to you in a guilt-free way.

WHAT HAVE THEY GOT TO DO WITH FINDING MY PURPOSE?

These tests will show you patterns of words and phrases that can be woven into your purpose if they are not there already. If the same words keep arising and they are not already in your purpose statement, you may want to revisit it and see if they belong there.

WHERE TO DO THE TESTS

There are a number of different websites that offer these tests. Search 'strengths tests', 'passions tests' or 'values tests' and find one or two from the selection that suit your schedule and budget. These are three of the ones I took that were free at the time of writing this book:

- Strengths: VIA Strengths Finder - viacharacter.org (highly recommended)
- Passions: GeniusU - passiontest.geniusu.com
- Values: Barrett Value Centre - valuescentre.com

TEST RESULTS - STRENGTHS, PASSIONS AND VALUES

_____

_____

_____

_____

_____

_____

_____

Phew!

I hope you have done at least some of the above tests. They are a useful tool to know yourself a little better, help refine your purpose and, of course, they can be a bit of fun as well.

If this has energized you, then flip to the next chapter and answer some of the deep questions about 'life, the universe and everything'.

If you wish to the look at my test results, check Appendix Two.

Purpose Statements

> Shona: *The purpose of my life is to be fun and impact positively on others.*

> Corey: *The purpose of my life is to connect and inspire people to be the best versions of themselves.*

> Jennifer: *The purpose of my life is to be my authentic self, to live with love and joy in my heart and to serve.*

> Rebecca: *The purpose of my life is to be authentic, kind and grow my own edges in order to empower others to be real and have a roll-on effect of creating greater understanding and unity in the world.*

MY PURPOSE STATEMENT

The purpose of my life is to

_____

_____

_____

_____

_____

9

DIVING DEEPER: QUESTIONS

 'Efforts and courage are not enough without purpose and direction.' – John F. Kennedy

Q&A

Below are questions that give you a good insight into YOU. By answering them you will see patterns of words plus phrases and notions that keep repeating. All the questions focus on your passions, strengths, and values plus what kind of impact or legacy you want to make.

The first step is to answer the questions, and the second step is to notice and highlight the main themes that emerge.

Put aside up to an hour, have no distractions and an open mind. You can tap your answers into your phone or type on a computer, but most people find an old-fashioned pen and paper works best for this. Handwriting seems to bypass a critical part of your brain. Some people write long-form paragraphs. Others prefer bullet points. Mind maps are often used. Do what feels right to you. The method you use to jot down the answers is not as important as the answers are.

You do not have to answer every question, but if you are resistant to answering a particular question, it can mean there is something important to dig out. There are a handful of questions per topic and some of them are similar but the different way they are written may just prompt an insightful answer. Write down whatever comes up without judgment. Remember, you don't have to show this to anyone.

Once the timer for writing finishes or you feel a natural conclusion, read over your answers and highlight common words and ideas. Check these against your purpose. Does your purpose statement reflect these in its own short way? If so, great. If not, look at tweaking it a little.

These questions are useful not just for refining your purpose but also for tapping into yourself, writing out your goals and so directing your future through your daily activities—what to say yes and no to. This will be discussed more in Chapter Eleven.

Remember to take some deep breaths, release tension in your body and smile. Now you are in a great state to begin this challenging but ultimately satisfying undertaking. Let's start!

Childhood Questions

- What did you love doing as a child?
- What did you want to be when you grew up? Why?
- What were you good at doing as a child and teenager?
- What are your most treasured memories from childhood?
- Think back to when you were younger: what just lit you up?
- What were your dreams when you were a child (say at 10 years old)?
- Have any passions stayed with you from childhood to adulthood? What ones?

CHILDHOOD ANSWERS

_____

_____

_____

_____

_____

_____

PAST QUESTIONS

- What parts of your life are you most satisfied with?
- What are the greatest moments of achievement or fulfillment in your life?
- What are some challenges, difficulties and hardships you have overcome?
- Excluding the major events of your life, what are three of your best memories?

PAST ANSWERS

_____

_____

_____

Flow Questions

- What activities make you lose track of time?
- What were you doing last time you lost yourself in an activity?
- Remember when things felt on a roll or effortless: what were you doing?
- When was the last time you experienced a sense of timelessness and flow?

Flow Answers

No Pay Questions

- What doesn't feel like work?
- What would you do even if nobody paid you?
- What would you do for a year if money were not an object?
- What would you spend time doing if you had complete financial abundance to do anything (after the mandatory 'hammock on the beach' period, of course)?

No Pay Answers

_____

_____

_____

_____

_____

_____

Fearless Questions

- If you were afraid of nothing, what would you do?
- What have you not tried because of your fear of failure or fear of success?
- Is there something that terrifies you but has always secretly captivated you?

FEARLESS ANSWERS

_____

_____

_____

_____

_____

LIKE OR LOVE QUESTIONS

- What types of books do you read?
- What documentaries or films do you watch?
- What are you curious about or interested in?
- What do you love to do but hardly ever make time for?
- What subject could you read 10 books about without getting bored?

LIKE OR LOVE ANSWERS

_____

_____

_____

_____

_____

_____

_____

ENERGIZED QUESTIONS

- What drives you? Why?
- What tasks make you feel most energized?
- When was the last time you felt true excitement? Why?
- What gets you up in the morning and makes you feel most alive?
- What are the places, people and events that make you feel energized?

ENERGIZED ANSWERS

_____

_____

_____

_____

_____

_____

_____

Joy Questions

- What are your most prized possessions? Why?
- What is something that can bring you to tears of joy?
- What activities do you absolutely love in your personal life?
- What makes you smile (people, events, hobbies, projects, etc.)?

Joy Answers

_____

_____

_____

_____

_____

_____

Role Model Questions

- Who do you look up to and why?
- What characteristics do you most admire in people?
- Who is living the life you want, and who can you model/emulate?
- Who inspires you the most and why (friends, authors, artists, leaders, etc.)?

ROLE MODEL ANSWERS

_____

_____

_____

_____

_____

STRENGTHS QUESTIONS

- What do you feel qualified to teach others?
- What do people always seem to ask you to help them with?
- What are you naturally good at (skills, abilities, talents, etc.)?
- What things do you do easily that seem to be difficult for other people?

STRENGTHS ANSWERS

_____

_____

_____

_____

Uniqueness Questions

- What things do you feel you are greatest at?
- What is the unique ability or gift you bring to the world?
- What do you do differently from everyone else that makes you stand out?
- What tools, technologies or online applications do you know how to use better than anyone else?

Uniqueness Answers

Work Questions

- What are the greatest sources of joy in your work?
- In what areas of work do you seem to get the best results?
- Where at work do you feel most confident and socially adept?

Work Answers

_____

_____

_____

_____

_____

_____

_____

Future Questions

- What would you still like to achieve in life?
- What would you like your future memories to be?
- What would you regret not fully doing, being or having in your life?
- What do you currently not have in your life that you would appreciate having?

FUTURE ANSWERS

_____

_____

_____

_____

_____

_____

_____

PROBLEM QUESTIONS

- What would you struggle for?
- What do you care about or what bothers you?
- What problems in the world do you want to fix?

PROBLEM ANSWERS

_____

_____

_____

_____

_____

Find Your Purpose in 15 Minutes WORKBOOK

_____

_____

Importance Questions

- What matters most to you? Why?
- What is most important that you take for granted?
- What positive, uplifting, inspiring quotes do you refer to?
- What things do you care most deeply about and that transcend your immediate desires?

Importance Answers

_____

_____

_____

_____

_____

_____

Destiny Questions

- What do you want your life to be about?
- What kind of person do you ultimately want to become?

- What goals need to be accomplished to get the kind of life you want?
- If you could get one single message to your children, your friends and family or a large group of people, what would it be?

DESTINY ANSWERS

_____

_____

_____

_____

_____

_____

_____

DOUBLE PHEW!

What a ride! These questions often bring up a whole heap of emotions. There may be tears. This is a good thing. You are tapping into the real you, and that is the only way you can really lean into your destiny.

Is your purpose statement feeling even more alive and relevant now? Good. That may give you the push you need to complete the exercises in the next chapter.

Purpose Statements

Melody: *The purpose of my life is to share love with others.*

Rita: *The purpose of my life is to be curious, joyful and healthy so that I can connect with and nurture others to contribute positively to my community.*

Diana: *The purpose of my life is to be healthy and full of life and to create abundance so that I can help others and can give my children all the tools they need to create their own happy and fulfilling lives.*

Valerie: *The purpose of my life is to live a wholesome life of my dreams, filled with magic of gratefulness and creation so that I can be the best of myself, charged and healthy and brave, open to wealth, freedom, wisdom, power and clarity, to be able to illuminate and make a difference around me and in the world.*

My Purpose Statement

The purpose of my life is to

_____

_____

_____

_____

10

DIVING DEEPER: EXERCISES

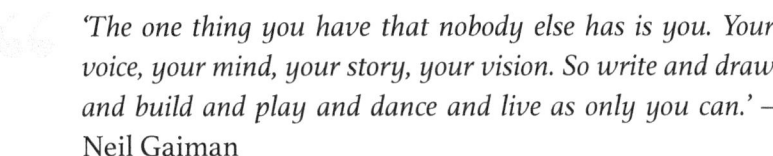 *'The one thing you have that nobody else has is you. Your voice, your mind, your story, your vision. So write and draw and build and play and dance and live as only you can.'* – Neil Gaiman

The Riches

You thought the questions were the hard part? Nup, sorry. They just scratched the surface. These exercises are challenging but boy do they dive down deep and bring up the greatest of treasures.

Take some deep breaths, shake your body out and try them if you dare…

1. Your Ideal Life Exercise

Imagine you are living your ideal life, five, ten or twenty years from now. Give yourself 20 minutes and write out a description (writing by hand is recommended) of your perfect day where you are not on vacation, just a 'normal' day in your ideal life. To prompt you, answer these questions:

- What are you doing?
- What is a typical day like?
- What kind of work do you do?
- What have you accomplished?
- What things are you most proud of?
- Who and what do you have in your life?
- What do your home, family, work and relationships look like?

This exercise will tap into what you love, what is important to you and what kind of legacy you want to leave behind.

Look for themes and patterns in what you have written and check back in with your purpose statement. Does your purpose light the way to your ideal life?

IDEAL LIFE EXERCISE

_____

_____

_____

_____

_____

_____

_____

_____

_____

_____

_____

_____

_____

_____

_____

_____

2. WHAT WHAT WHAT EXERCISE

For some people, even with the quick purpose exercise, the tests and the questions, a true purpose may remain elusive or not feel exactly right. This exercise is designed to extract it out, kicking and screaming if need be!

To get to your big WHY it has been argued that you shouldn't ask more 'why' questions but instead ask a series of WHAT questions.

Start with something, it could be big or small, that is important to you. Then ask:

> What about X is important to me?

For example:

- What about keeping fit is important to me?
- What about being a great parent is important to me?
- What about having a successful business is important to me?

Then write out the first thing that comes into your head as a response to that question. I did this exercise for the 'keeping fit' question:

1. What about keeping fit is important to me?

> Answer: Keeping fit is important to me as I have more energy when I am fitter.

Then use the answer you have written down and ask the first question again: What about X is important to me? For example:

2. What about having more energy is important to me?

> Answer: Having more energy is important to me as I am able to do the work I want and be there for my family.

Here's the kicker—you need to keep asking this WHAT question at least FIVE to SEVEN times!

The first few answers will come from your head, but the next few will challenge you to be radically honest and come from your heart. This will almost always uncover something personal, genuine and fundamental about what drives you.

Even if you start with something small, by the time you are at least five layers deep you will find a very deep WHY for what you want to do. You will naturally arrive at your destination—your ultimate purpose.

Let's continue with my 'What What What' example for keeping fit:

3. What about doing the work I want and being there for my family is important to me?

>Answer: I can feel successful in my work and home life.

4. What about feeling successful in my work and home life is important to me?

>Answer: If I am successful I can inspire others to live their lives well.

5. What about inspiring others is important to me?

>Answer: I can contribute to making the world a better place.

6. What about making the world a better place is important to me?

>Answer: I will live well knowing that I have done my best.

Once you feel you have reached a natural end to the 'What What What' questions, check your five-to-seven-layer-deep 'what' answer to your purpose statement derived from the 15-minute exercise.

Do they marry up? Sometimes how much they correspond is uncanny.

Or do you need to refine your purpose slightly to incorporate this new understanding of yourself?

This is my purpose statement:

>'The purpose of my life is to be my best self, full of love, energy and fun ('sparkle'), so I can continue to learn and create and then inspire others to achieve their potential'.

Obviously doing my best or being my best self is extremely important to me. Mmmm, interesting.

What What What Exercise

_____

_____

_____

_____

_____

_____

_____

_____

_____

_____

_____

_____

3. Write Your Own Obituary Exercise

The obituary exercise asks you to fast forward to the end of your life and then imagine that you are looking back over your time here on Earth.

This works as a prompt as it stimulates urgency that the end of your life may be nearer than you think. This sounds a little morbid, but it will help pinpoint any areas for change and perhaps jolt you into action.

You do not have to follow the traditional format for an obituary. Think of it more as a prompt to define your ideal life and legacy. This exercise could also be called 'Write Your Own Eulogy', 'Write Your 100th Birthday Speech' or 'Write a Letter to Your Grandkids from Your Rocking Chair'.

Don't get caught up in the semantics of what this exercise is called. Choose whichever works for you. It is the imagining of your big picture life that is the important part here.

Paint a picture of the person you want to be, of a life well lived. Look back at your life and all that you've achieved and acquired, all the relationships you have developed and what matters the most to you. Be specific and detailed but also grandiose.

Review different areas of your life such as health, family, work and contribution. Use words that inspire you. Start with what you have already accomplished and are proud of, and then move into your ambitions for the ideal future you.

Answer questions such as:

- Who have you impacted?
- What legacy are you leaving?
- What are you known or remembered for?
- What characteristics and qualities do you have?
- What are your quirks and charming idiosyncrasies?

- What specific things did you achieve in your lifetime?

If you are finding it hard to write all your positive attributes, greatest accomplishments and what you would be fondly remembered for, then ask yourself how you would NOT want to be thought of. What goals would you regret not having achieved?

What would you NOT want on your headstone?

I found the best way to do this was to write non-stop for at least three to ten minutes, answering the questions above and then adding anything else I thought of. Afterwards, I rewrote it all so it sounded like an obituary, organizing it so it highlighted what I enjoyed and achieved in the different areas of my life. See what I wrote as my obituary in Appendix Three.

Not only is this a valuable exercise to revisit your purpose statement, it is also an opportunity to get back on track, refocus your priorities and resurrect dreams that have become lost in the daily grind.

OBITUARY EXERCISE

_____

_____

_____

_____

_____

Find Your Purpose in 15 Minutes WORKBOOK

TRIPLE PHEW!

Didn't you have a blast getting to know yourself better?

What were the guts of it all? Do the patterns and themes that emerge from the tests, questions and exercises reflect your original purpose statement?

The odd person does a massive rewrite of their purpose, but most people say that they are happy with their 15-minute purpose statement, perhaps with a few minor tweaks here and there.

The final two chapters show you how you can supercharge your purpose plus explain why finding your purpose benefits us all.

PURPOSE STATEMENTS

> PJ: *The purpose of my life is to learn, discover and gain wisdom to empower my loved ones and serve others.*
>
> **Haidee:** *The purpose of my life is to be authentic and real, and to care and be there for others when they need it.*
>
> Jenny: *The purpose of my life is to enjoy creating mindfully, so I can write encouraging connection amongst older women.*
>
> Nandani: *The purpose of my life is to be playful, loving, be passionate, be grateful, to grow so that I can help, serve, empower and make a difference to the world I live in.*

MY PURPOSE STATEMENT

The purpose of my life is to

_____

_____

_____

_____

11

SUPERCHARGE YOUR PURPOSE

 'I realized there are two things you take with you when you die. The love you've shared and the difference you've made.'
– Jane Seymour

WHAT ELSE IS THERE?

You have your purpose statement, you believe it and are starting to live it. You may even have tackled the last three chapters and learned about yourself, your character and your motivations more deeply. Perhaps you used the additional information to tweak or add to your original 15-minute purpose statement.

What else can you possibly use your purpose statement and the greater understanding of inner workings for?

This chapter gives you two main options to supercharge your purpose. These are extras and there is no requirement to take them on, but if you are feeling energized with all this reflection work, you may want to attempt these two supercharging activities.

Purpose and Growth

An earlier chapter touched on the Six Human Needs and noted that the two secondary needs for growth and contribution are often not met as the four primary needs for certainty, variety, significance and love take precedence, especially your need for certainty.

One of the secondary needs is for growth. Although growth is evident everywhere from trees to babies, in this area it refers to using your strengths and abilities to work towards something, create something or improve yourself.

Growth is a natural force in the world and although many people resist it, we need it. As Victor Frankl states in *Man's Search for Meaning*: "What a man needs is not a tensionless state but rather the striving and struggling for a worthwhile goal, a freely chosen task."

Finding your purpose can be the catalyst to your much-needed growth. One way a purpose assists personal growth is to give you a tangible concept to refer to when you embark on goal setting.

For exactly why and how to set goals, I recommend reading my book, *Super Sexy Goal Setting*. Here is a quick summary to get you started: decide on four goals for the next 12 months. These should be exciting and meaningful to you (i.e.: 'sexy'). If you like, make a goal about each of the following: health, relationships, work/business and fun/just for you.

When you write out your goals make sure they align with your purpose statement. Now you have four super sexy goals that are aligned with your need for growth and with your purpose.

> If that is not supercharged, I don't know what is.

Purpose and Contribution

You attain a meaningful life from a connection to a wider cause. In other words, by fulfilling the last of your six human needs, your need for contribution. The impact part of your purpose statement may be as simple as 'sharing my gifts with the world' or 'inspiring others'.

In order to supercharge your purpose for the contribution part, here is a simple way to make it crystal clear exactly WHO you want to serve and HOW you will help them. Note that you may or may not be paid for this service to the world.

Answer these three questions:

1. What do you like to do in which you have at least some expertise? Some call this their '10,000 hours skill', but I don't think you have to reach that level of mastery.
2. What does the community, tribe or audience that you want to impact need and want? In other words, what pain do they need healed? Or what joy would benefit them the most?
3. How are those people helped, or how do they transform or improve as a result of your contribution?

My answers:

1. Write books
2. Busy people who want more from life
3. Gain tools and wisdom to reach their potential

Then put it all together using a 'two-minute elevator pitch' role definition template that clearly states what you do and who benefits:

> I (your expertise) that help (description of people you help) so that they (transformation)

My two-minute elevator pitch:

I write books that help busy people who want more from life so that they gain tools and wisdom to reach their potential.

The answers to these questions can and will change over time, so look at updating your two-minute elevator pitch each year when you review your purpose statement and write out your annual goals.

HOW WILL YOU SUPERCHARGE YOUR PURPOSE?

Write down the supercharging ideas from above that resonate most with you and add in any of your own.

_____

_____

_____

_____

_____

_____

_____

_____

_____

_____

Purpose Statements

Natalie: *The purpose of my life is to be happy, to enjoy and appreciate every moment, so that I can empower and love others unconditionally.*

Edyta: *The purpose of my life is to be healthy, happy and have freedom so that I can grow, create and achieve, and then inspire other people to success.*

Sue: *The purpose of my life is to be positive, live with meaning and purpose, give support and help to others by inspiring wellbeing, enjoy the loved ones who provide so much joy.*

Rach: *The purpose of my life is to achieve massive success, with sheer determination, whilst maintaining peace and honoring my soul, I in turn share my gifts with others to empower, inspire and assist them to fulfill their dreams.*

My Purpose Statement

The purpose of my life is to

_____

_____

_____

_____

12

WHAT IS THE PURPOSE OF A BOOK ON PURPOSE?

'Happiness is like a butterfly, the more you chase it, the more it will evade you, but if you notice the other things around you, it will gently come and sit on your shoulder.' – Henry David Thoreau

Know Thyself

The purpose of this book about finding your purpose (very meta!) is simple: to help you to know yourself better.

Sure, a 15-minute exercise to find your purpose may not be the deepest navel-gazing you will ever do, but it is a start. You may never look at your purpose again, but if you have discovered one more thing about yourself that helps you live better, then this book has met its purpose.

Of course, I would love everyone to not only find a purpose, believe it and start living it, but also do the other tasks—the tests, questions and exercises. These allow you to take some time checking in and getting to know yourself better.

I truly believe that understanding the core of you will help in your life, relationships and work.

As author and businesswoman, Arianna Huffington states in *Thrive*: "We are not on this earth to accumulate victories or trophies but to be whittled down until what is left is who we truly are."

BENEFITS OF HAVING A PURPOSE FOR YOU

You may have already noticed some of the benefits of having a purpose such as:

- You feel more certain in yourself as you become more focused on what you want to be and clear about what you really want to do.
- You have a sense of direction, a path, an exciting journey to a meaningful destination.
- A purpose gets you out of bed with resilience and energy that come from within.
- Having a purpose means living for today, not for some end game, or even worse, someone else's game.
- A purpose allows you to be more compassionate to both yourself and others.
- Purpose is a primary key to strong mental health as you know you are here for a reason.
- Your purpose leads to healing and fulfillment as you feel like your life is about something bigger than just yourself.

As Jen Sincero says in *You are a Badass*: "It is about getting clear on what makes you happy and what makes you feel most alive and then creating that instead of pretending you can't have it or don't deserve it."

BENEFITS OF HAVING A PURPOSE FOR THE WORLD

Having a purpose with a contribution element has an immeasurable effect on the world. There is only one unique YOU. You are the only YOU there ever will be. It makes no sense to hide, to play small and to not be generous.

There is absolutely no doubt the world is improved by you sharing your gifts.

Don't deny the world your magnificence. We are not here to fit in but to be different and add a small piece of ourselves to the mosaic of life. Add service to your life. People want to be part of something that makes a difference. I envisage that if everyone operates from their truest passions, strengths and values, the world will be a better place.

Media company CEO, Tim O'Reilly couldn't have said it any better: "Pursue something so important that even if you fail, the world is better off with you having tried."

THE TRUTH

The truth is that it doesn't actually matter whether you know for sure if you are living your real purpose in life.

The truth is that living deliberately leads in a roundabout way to true happiness.

The truth is that life is NOT short. Life is the longest thing we have. It is disrespectful to not at least try and make it the masterpiece we wish it to be.

When you decide to show up, take action and do some good in the world it is almost impossible for love, joy and success not to accompany you on your purpose-driven journey.

Dream big. Laugh often. Take a deep breath and just have a go.

Your Purpose Statement

Here is my purpose again:

The purpose of my life is to be my best self, full of love, energy and fun ('sparkle'), so I can continue to learn and create and then inspire others to achieve their potential.

What is your purpose? I would love to hear it. If you want to share it with me, shoot me a quick email: julie@julieschooler.com.

My Purpose Statement

The purpose of my life is to

_____

_____

_____

_____

_____

FIND YOUR PURPOSE IN 15 MINUTES WORKBOOK - ADDITIONAL NOTES

APPENDIX ONE – FIND YOUR PURPOSE IN 15 MINUTES SUMMARY

Purpose Recap

Your purpose is your WHY for being here. It is what you live for, what is important to you and what makes your life significant and worthwhile.

A purpose statement should be short, positive and powerfully resonate with you. The template below is a useful foundation that can also be rearranged to fit your unique purpose statement.

> **Definition:** Your purpose is about who you want to BE and what you want to DO so that you have an IMPACT on others.
>
> **Template:** 'The purpose of my life is to (be and/or do) _____ to (impact) _____.'

E.g.: The purpose of my life is to be courageous, abundance-oriented and full of gratitude so that I can share my gifts with others and help the environment.

Appendix One – Find Your Purpose in 15 Minutes Summary

E.g.: The purpose of my life is to be full of passion so I can use my determination and inquisitive nature to help to make a difference in my community and the world.

The Words Lists

One of the most difficult parts of finding your purpose is coming up with the right words to use. The 15-minute purpose exercise makes things super easy for you by giving you all the words you need for the BE, DO and IMPACT elements.

Use any of the words. They are displayed in a manner that is meant to make them easier to read and choose, not because the 'main' word is more important than the associated words and phrases.

Feel free to highlight all the words you like. Then try and narrow down to the most important ones for you. It is okay to drop a few of the words when writing out your purpose statement. They won't mind.

You may need to change the words slightly to fit into your purpose statement ('love' to 'loving', 'create' to 'creative', 'power' to 'powerful', etc.).

If you have a word not in the lists that best suits your purpose, please use it. People say these lists nudge them to come up with other words, or they add a faith-based component as well.

Find Your Purpose in 15 Minutes Instructions

1. Take a deep breath and say in an excited voice: 'I will find my purpose today!'

2. Keep this purpose statement template in mind:

   'The purpose of my life is to (be and/or do) _____ to (impact) _____'

Appendix One – Find Your Purpose in 15 Minutes Summary

3. Read **The Fab List** below and highlight or write down any words that resonate the most with you.

Most people eventually settle on between 2 and 8 words:

- Love – nice, kind, caring, grace
- Healthy – energy, vitality, wellbeing, fit, strong
- Happy – joy, cheerful, positive, optimistic, fulfilled
- Fun – enjoy, playful, humor, laughter
- Grow – learn, discover, improve, master, knowledge
- Achieve – accomplish, success, excellence, live my dreams
- Create – imagine, innovate, invent, art
- Courage – brave, confident, bold, adventurous, face fear
- Passionate – excitement, enthusiastic, zest for life
- Give – help, contribute, serve, generous, benevolent
- Peace – calm, simplicity, tranquil, serene, rest
- Curious – inquisitive, interested, wonder, be in awe
- Spiritual – aware, conscious, wholeness, mindful, transcendent
- Integrity – fair, honest, sincere, true, open
- Authentic – real, genuine, be me, be myself, be true to me
- Ideal self – be my best self, reach my potential, be a good person
- Appreciate – gratitude, grateful, thankful, treasure
- Compassionate – supportive, considerate, empathetic, thoughtful, warm
- Persistent – determined, driven, motivated, ambitious, grit
- Abundance – wealth, freedom, beauty, wisdom, power

4. Read the **Impact Lists** below and highlight or write down the verbs and nouns that fit the impact part of your purpose statement.

Most people choose between 1 and 3 words from each list:

Verbs

- Give – help, gift, provide, give abundance to
- Share – serve, share my gifts, contribute, nourish, delight
- Connect – teach, write, speak, learn, read
- Lead – empower, inspire, encourage, spread magic, focus on
- Accept – listen, understand, heal, forgive
- Make a difference – give hope to, work towards, stand for, challenge

Nouns

- Non-specific – others, humans, all beings, people, creatures
- Specific – organizations, causes, charities, community, groups
- Friends and Family – loved ones, my family, my children, my tribe
- General – the world, the environment, nature, my legacy

5. Take out a pen and paper and write out

   'The purpose of my life is to ____'

6. Add your favorite words from **The Fab List** and the **Impact Lists** into the template and rewrite your purpose statement until it powerfully resonates with you. This may take a handful of attempts but you WILL get there.

7. Read your final purpose statement aloud.

Congratulations, just like that you have found your purpose!

APPENDIX TWO – MY TEST RESULTS

I took the tests discussed in Chapter Eight, so if you are curious about my test results, here are the main ones:

Myers-Briggs Type Indicator (MBTI) Personality Test

Test taken via 16personalities.com – free during the writing of this book

Current test result: ENFJ

Previously identified with INFJ and ISFJ

Kolbe A Index

Test taken via kolbe.com – currently US$50

My Kolbe action style: High on 'Fact finder' and 'Follow through'

The Four Tendencies Quiz

Test taken via quiz.gretchenrubin.com - free during the writing of this book

Tendency: Upholder

The 5 Love Languages Profile

Test taken via 5lovelanguages.com - free during the writing of this book

Love language: Quality Time and Words of Affirmation

The VIA Strengths Finder

Test taken via viacharacter.org - free during the writing of this book

Top three highest strengths: love of learning, gratitude, industry, diligence and perseverance

Top three lowest strengths: bravery and valor, modesty and humility, forgiveness and mercy

APPENDIX THREE – MY OBITUARY EXERCISE

Julie lived to a ripe old age and accomplished a lot over her lifetime. She truly lived her life with purpose, motivated to be her best self, full of sparkle, and used her gifts to encourage others to do the same.

She valued and exuded the following qualities wherever she could: love, joy, contribution, beauty, inspiration, wisdom, energy, health, integrity, fun, creativity, success and abundance.

Health and fitness were important to Julie—she enjoyed challenging herself to be as strong and as full of energy as she could so she could keep up with her work commitments… and her grandkids!

Having meaningful relationships as a wife, mama, sister, daughter, friend or business colleague were of utmost value. Spending time with family and friends was a major part of Julie's life. She loved fun days at the beautiful locations near where she lived and the events, dinners and casual get-togethers that she often arranged.

Julie started writing and publishing books out of an innate drive to be creative after her first child was born. This developed into a successful business through which Julie was constantly learning and sharing wisdom about life, love and what is truly important via blogging, courses, speaking and coaching.

She loved seeing how creative she could be so also wrote children's picture books, novels and turned out other products that were imaginative, beautiful and fun.

Travel was a great love and Julie travelled extensively, visiting exotic places and relaxing in many tropical locations. Her kids still remember that fantastic Disneyland holiday when they were young, and her best friends fondly remember her 50th birthday celebrations across France—a lot of champagne was consumed on that trip!

Everyone knows how much Julie loved going after and achieving meaningful goals. She especially liked checking things off her long bucket list. The 40 things she checked off her 'Top40 Bucket List' the year she turned 40 were just the start.

Although she worked hard, Julie also made time for fun as she knew it was the key to a fulfilling life. She enjoyed indulging in doorstop novels, going to the cinema, dancing like an idiot and playing with her children and grandchildren. She sometimes showed her dark sense of humor and also loved being ridiculously silly on occasion.

Having an abundance mindset was a major focus of Julie's and she contributed to the world in a myriad of ways—giving to charity, helping out in the community and always having a listening ear plus a cup of tea or glass of wine ready for family, friends or other mamas when it was needed.

Julie always said she wanted to feel like that her life meant something. Her greatest wish was to leave her mark on the world so it would be a better place to live in simply due to the fact that she was here. I think we can all agree that her wish was granted.

READER GIFT: THE HAPPY20

There is no doubt that having a purpose will transform your life, but it is also important to remember to squeeze the best out every single day. To remind you of this, I created

THE HAPPY20
20 Free Ways to Boost Happiness in 20 Seconds or Less

A PDF gift for you with quick ideas to improve your mood and add a little sparkle to your day.

Head to **JulieSchooler.com/gift** and grab your copy today.

ABOUT THE AUTHOR

Julie had aspirations of being a writer since she was very young but somehow got sidetracked into the corporate world. After the birth of her first child, she rediscovered her creative side. You can find her at JulieSchooler.com.

Her *Easy Peasy* books provide simple and straightforward information on parenting topics. The *Nourish Your Soul* series shares delicious wisdom to feel calmer, happier and more fulfilled.

Busy people can avoid wasting time searching for often confusing and conflicting advice and instead spend time with the beautiful tiny humans in their lives and do what makes their hearts sing.

Julie lives with her family in a small, magnificent country at the bottom of the world where you may find her trying to bake the perfect chocolate brownie.

facebook.com/JulieSchoolerAuthor
instagram.com/julie.schooler
twitter.com/JulieSchooler

BOOKS BY JULIE SCHOOLER

Easy Peasy Books
Easy Peasy Potty Training

Easy Peasy Healthy Eating

Nourish Your Soul Books
Rediscover Your Sparkle

Crappy to Happy

Embrace Your Awesomeness

Bucket List Blueprint

Super Sexy Goal Setting

Find Your Purpose in 15 Minutes

Clutter-Free Forever

Children's Picture Books
Maxy-Moo Flies to the Moon

Collections
Change Your Life 3-in-1 Collection

Rebelliously Happy 3-in-1 Collection

Workbooks
Bucket List Blueprint Workbook

Super Sexy Goal Setting Workbook

Find Your Purpose in 15 Minutes Workbook

JulieSchooler.com/books

ACKNOWLEDGMENTS

I have huge appreciation for my dear friend, Kylie, who was the major contributor for the nihilistic rant in Chapter Three. Usually with the accompaniment of a few glasses of wine, we have been discussing whether life has any meaning at all for 25 years. Long may the debate continue.

Thanks to the 100 volunteers who put their hands up for the original 'Find Your Purpose' questionnaire. I was almost ready to give up on the whole project. Without your input and enthusiasm, this book simply would not have happened. Your purpose statements have moved me to tears. We have a lot of love and humanity worth sharing in this world.

To Andrew and our two beautiful tiny humans, Dylan and Eloise. I live in a perpetual state of astonishment about how fortunate my life is. Thank you for making me laugh every single day.

PLEASE LEAVE A REVIEW

Find Your Purpose in 15 Minutes

WORKBOOK

Your Shortcut to a Meaningful Life

THANK YOU FOR READING THIS BOOK

I devoted many months to researching and writing this book. I then spent more time having it professionally edited, working with a designer to create an awesome cover and launching it into the world.

Time, money and heart has gone into this book and I very much hope you enjoyed reading it as much as I loved creating it.

It would mean the world to me if you could spend a few minutes writing a review on Goodreads or the online store where you purchased this book.

A review can be as short or long as you like and should be helpful and honest to assist other potential buyers of the book.

Reviews provide social proof that people like and recommend the book. More book reviews mean more book sales which means I can write more books.

Your book review helps me, as an independent author, more than you could ever know. I read every single review and when I get five-star review it absolutely makes my day.

Thanks, Julie.

REFERENCES

People and Resources

Various TED and TEDx talks, podcasts and blogs on finding your purpose

Bluezones website

Tony Robbins

Martha Beck

Tim Ferriss

Marie Forleo

Chris Howard

Kurek Ashley

Adam Robinson

Elizabeth Gilbert

Brian Tracey

JP Sears

References

Alan Watts

Simon Sinek

Oprah Winfrey

...and many others

Books

Achieving Your Best Self – Fast Track Your Efforts to Achieving Your Highest Goals – Dr. David Barton (NZ, 2016)

Authentic Happiness – Using the New Positive Psychology to Realize Your Potential for Lasting Fulfillment – Martin Seligman, Ph.D. (US, 2002)

Feel the Fear and Do It Anyway – How to Turn Your Fear and Indecision into Confidence and Action – Susan Jeffers (UK, 1987)

Finding Your Own North Star – How to Claim the Life You Were Meant to Live – Martha Beck (US, 2001)

Finding Your Way in a Wild New World – Reclaim Your True Nature to Create the Life You Want – Martha Beck (US, 2012)

Find Your Why – A Practical Guide for Discovering Purpose for You and Your Team – Simon Sinek, David Mead, Peter Docker (US, 2017)

Life on Purpose – How Living for What Matters Most Changes Everything – Victor J. Strecher (US, 2016)

Man's Search for Meaning – Victor E. Frankl (US, 1959 / 2006)

Minimalism – Live a Meaningful Life – Joshua Fields Millburn and Ryan Nicodemus (US, 2016)

References

Start With Why – How Great Leaders Inspire Everyone to Take Action – Simon Sinek (US, 2009)

Steering by Starlight – The Science and Magic of Finding Your Destiny – Martha Beck (US, 2008)

The Destiny Formula – Find Your Purpose. Overcome Your Fear of Failure. Use Your Natural Talents and Strengths to Build a Successful Life – Ayodeji Awosika (US, 2015)

The Five Love Languages – The Secret to Love that Lasts – Gary Chapman (US, 1992 / 2010)

The Happiness of Pursuit – Finding the Quest that Will Bring Purpose to Your Life – Chris Guillebeau (US, 2014)

The Life You Were Born to Live – A Guide to Finding Your Life Purpose – Dan Millman (US, 1993)

The ONE Thing – The surprisingly simple truth behind extraordinary results – Gary Keller with Jay Papasan (US, 2013)

The Secret – Rhonda Byrne (US, 2006)

The Seven Habits of Highly Effective People – Restoring the Character Ethic – Steven R. Covey (US, 1990)

*The Subtle Art of Not Giving a F*ck – A Counterintuitive Approach to Living a Good Life* – Mark Manson (US, 2016)

The Top Five Regrets of the Dying – A Life Transformed by the Dearly Departed – Bronnie Ware (US, 2011)

The Winner's Bible – Rewire Your Brain for Permanent Change – Dr. Kerry Spackman (USA, 2009)

Thrive – The Third Metric to Redefining Success and Creating a Life of Wellbeing, Wisdom and Wonder – Arianna Huffington (US, 2014)

What Matters Most – Living a More Considered Life – James Hollis, PhD (US, 2009)

You are a Badass – How to Stop Doubting Your Greatness and Start Living an Awesome Life – Jen Sincero (US, 2013)

www.ingramcontent.com/pod-product-compliance
Lightning Source LLC
Chambersburg PA
CBHW072007290426
44109CB00018B/2160